Augel

Young
KATHERINE
JOHNSON

WILLIAM AUGEL
Story & Art

BENJAMIN CROZE
Translator

JONATHAN STEVENSON
English-Language Edition Editor

VINCENT HENRY & ALEX LECOCQ
Original Edition Editors

SANDY TANAKA
Designer

JERRY FRISSEN
Senior Art Director

FABRICE GIGER
Publisher

Special thanks to Espace des sciences, Michel Cabaret, Annie Forté, Christelle Massol, Margaux Massol and Michel Bouchet.

Rights and Licensing - licensing@humanoids.com
Press and Social Media - pr@humanoids.com

YOUNG KATHERINE JOHNSON. First printing. This book is a publication of Humanoids, Inc. 8033 Sunset Blvd. #628, Los Angeles, CA 90046.

Library of Congress Control Number: 2022945218

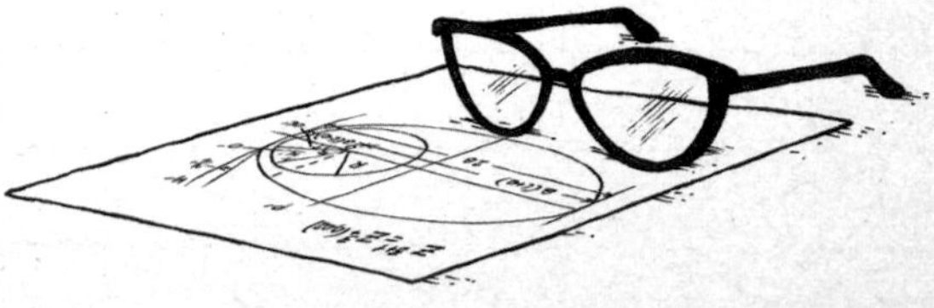

THE FAMILY

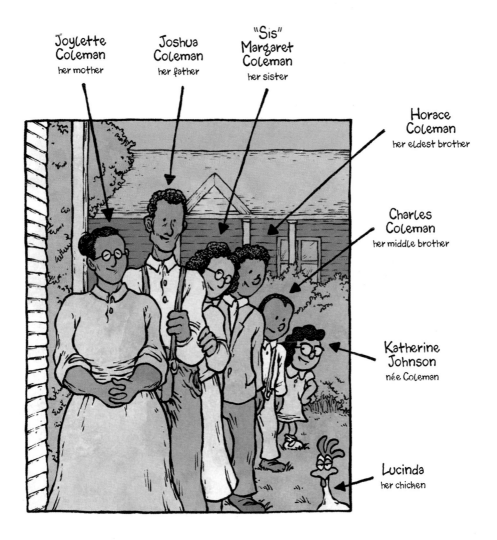

Joylette Coleman
her mother

Joshua Coleman
her father

"Sis" Margaret Coleman
her sister

Horace Coleman
her eldest brother

Charles Coleman
her middle brother

Katherine Johnson
née Coleman

Lucinda
her chichen

 ☆☆ This icon indicates that the page contains a mathematical puzzle for the reader to solve. The solutions can be found starting on page 66. The number of stars indicates the level of difficulty.

3267

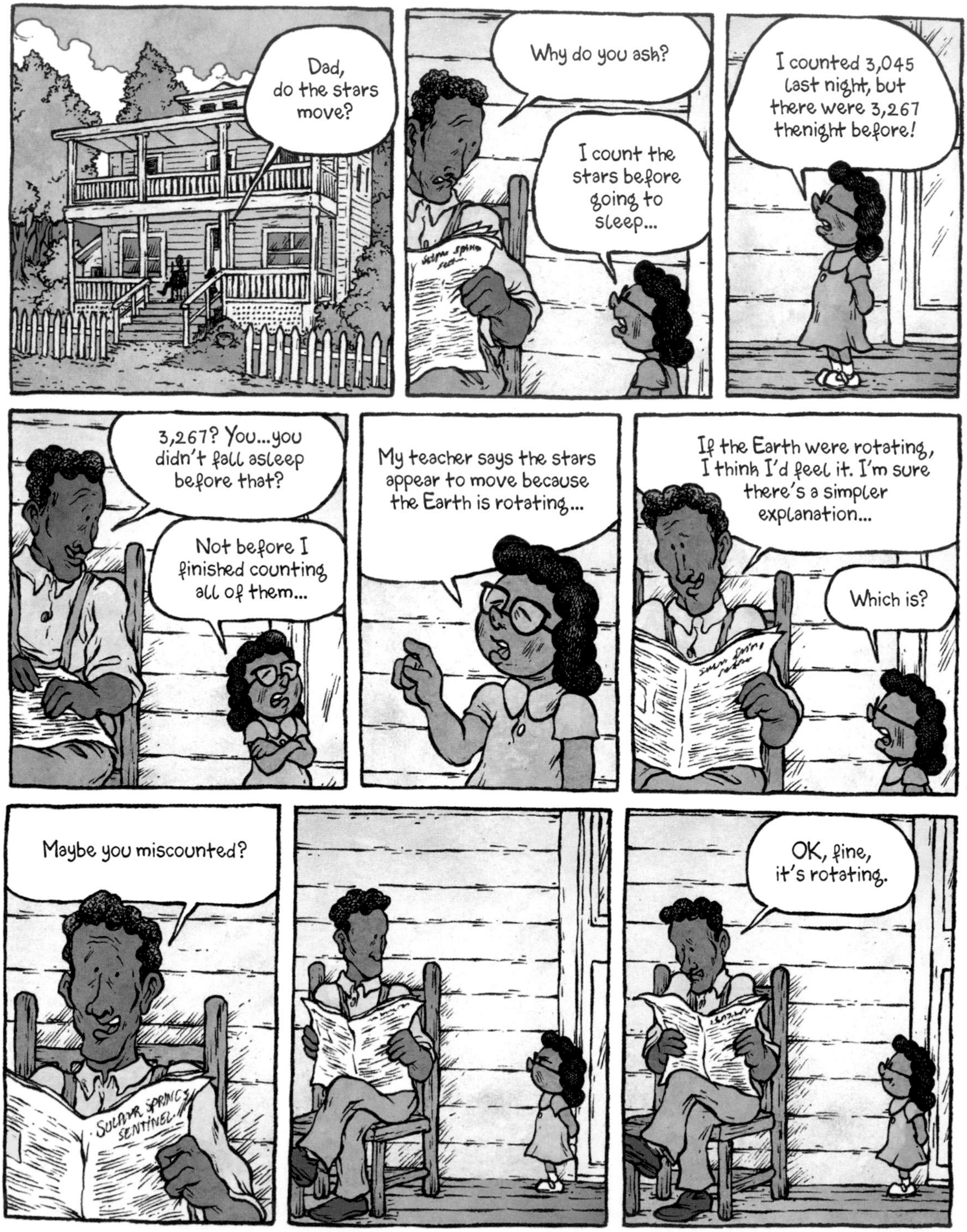

Dad, do the stars move?
Why do you ask?
I count the stars before going to sleep...
I counted 3,045 last night, but there were 3,267 thenight before!
3,267? You...you didn't fall asleep before that?
Not before I finished counting all of them...
My teacher says the stars appear to move because the Earth is rotating...
If the Earth were rotating, I think I'd feel it. I'm sure there's a simpler explanation...
Which is?
Maybe you miscounted?
OK, fine, it's rotating.

Mr. Coleman=Joshua=Papa

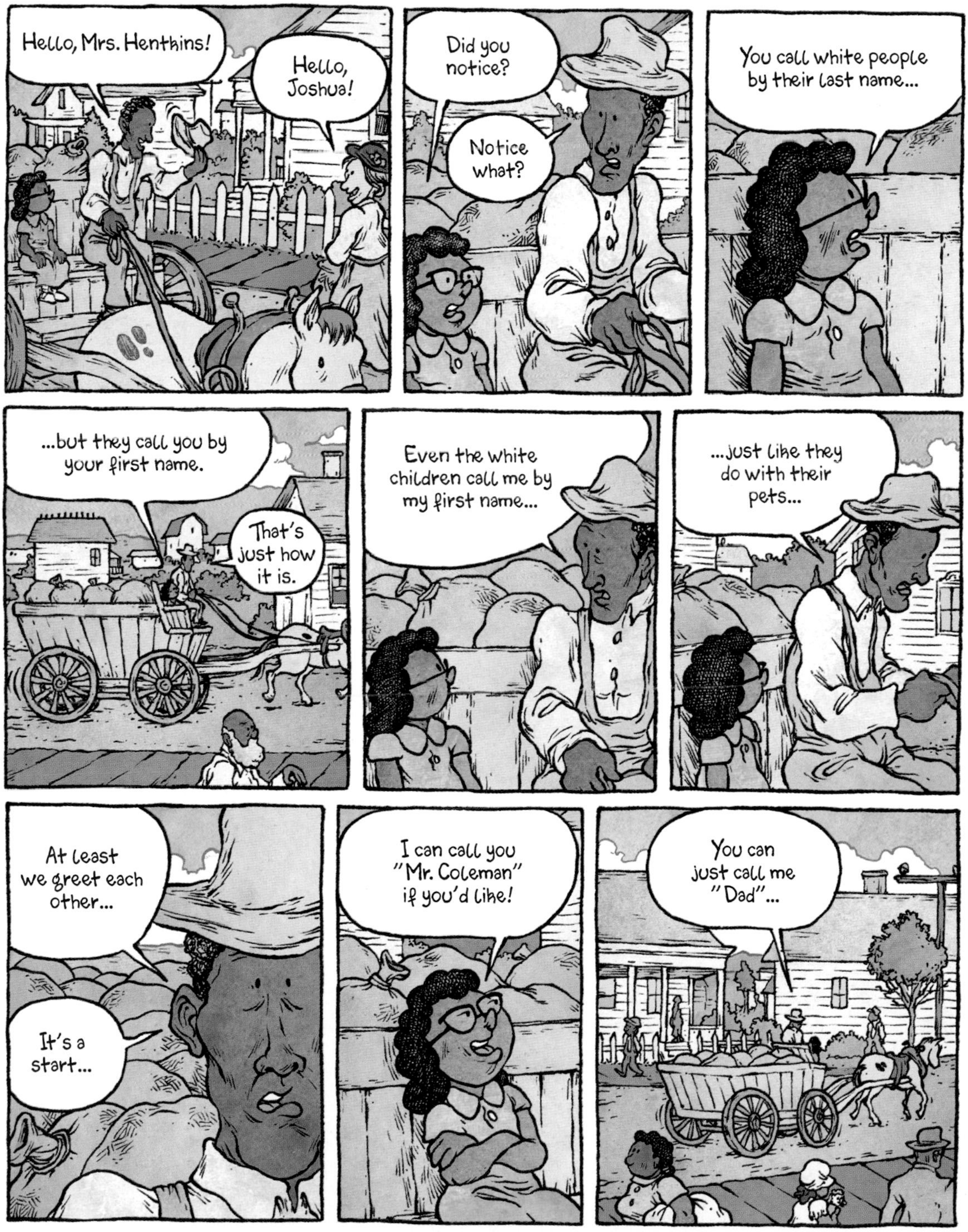
Hello, Mrs. Henthins!
Hello, Joshua!
Did you notice?
Notice what?
You call white people by their last name...
...but they call you by your first name.
That's just how it is.
Even the white children call me by my first name...
...just like they do with their pets...
At least we greet each other...
It's a start...
I can call you "Mr. Coleman" if you'd like!
You can just call me "Dad"...

But Mom, I can go to school, really!

I can still make it if I leave now!

If the school is half a mile away and I walk at a speed of 3 miles per hour...

...I can make it there by 9:15!

The numbers don't lie!

Out of the question! The doctor said you have a fever and have to stay in bed...

...a fever of 102°F. You're right, the numbers don't lie!

What time did Katherine wake up? (Answer on page 66)

7,000

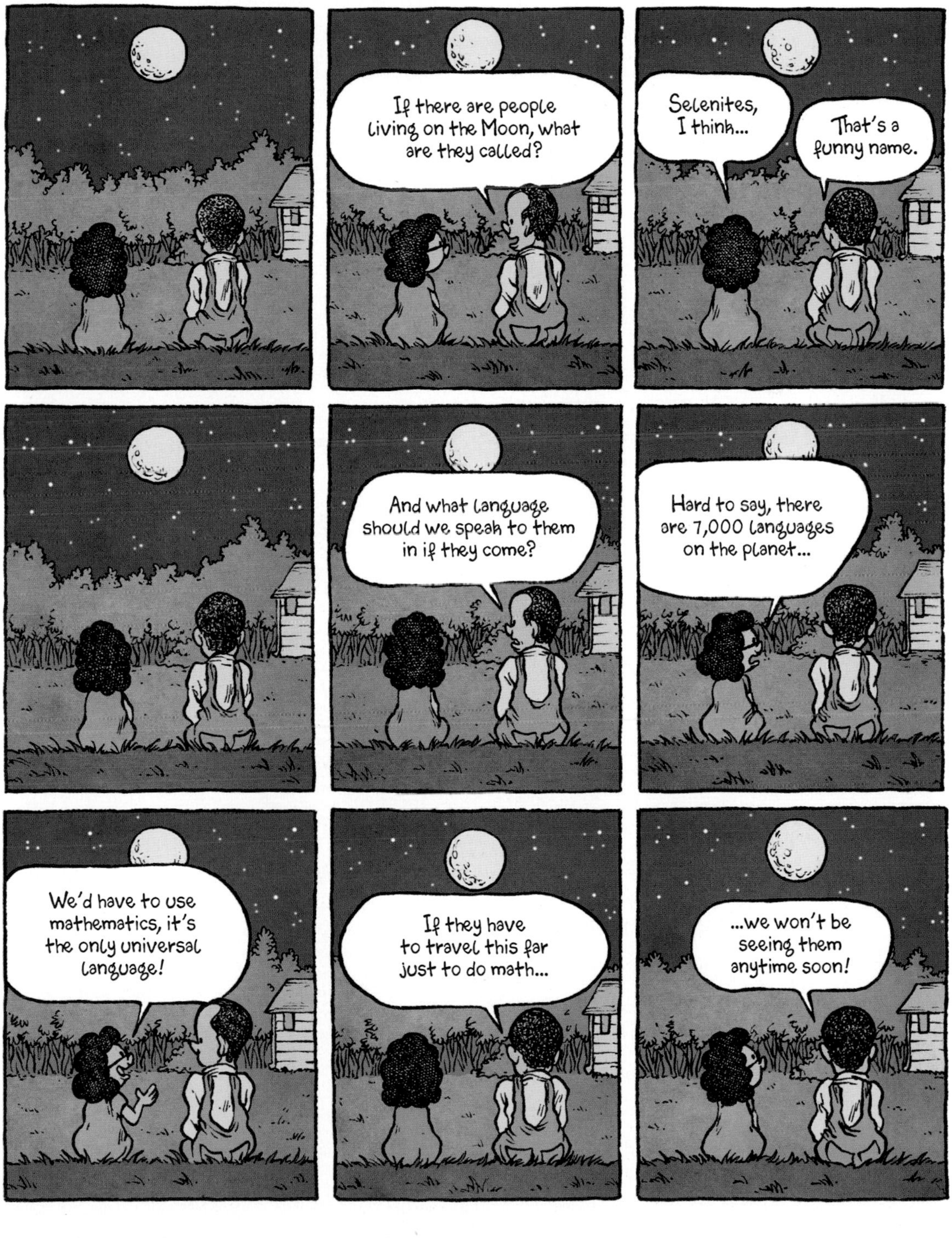
If there are people living on the Moon, what are they called?
Selenites, I think...
That's a funny name.
And what language should we speak to them in if they come?
Hard to say, there are 7,000 languages on the planet...
We'd have to use mathematics, it's the only universal language!
If they have to travel this far just to do math...
...we won't be seeing them anytime soon!

142

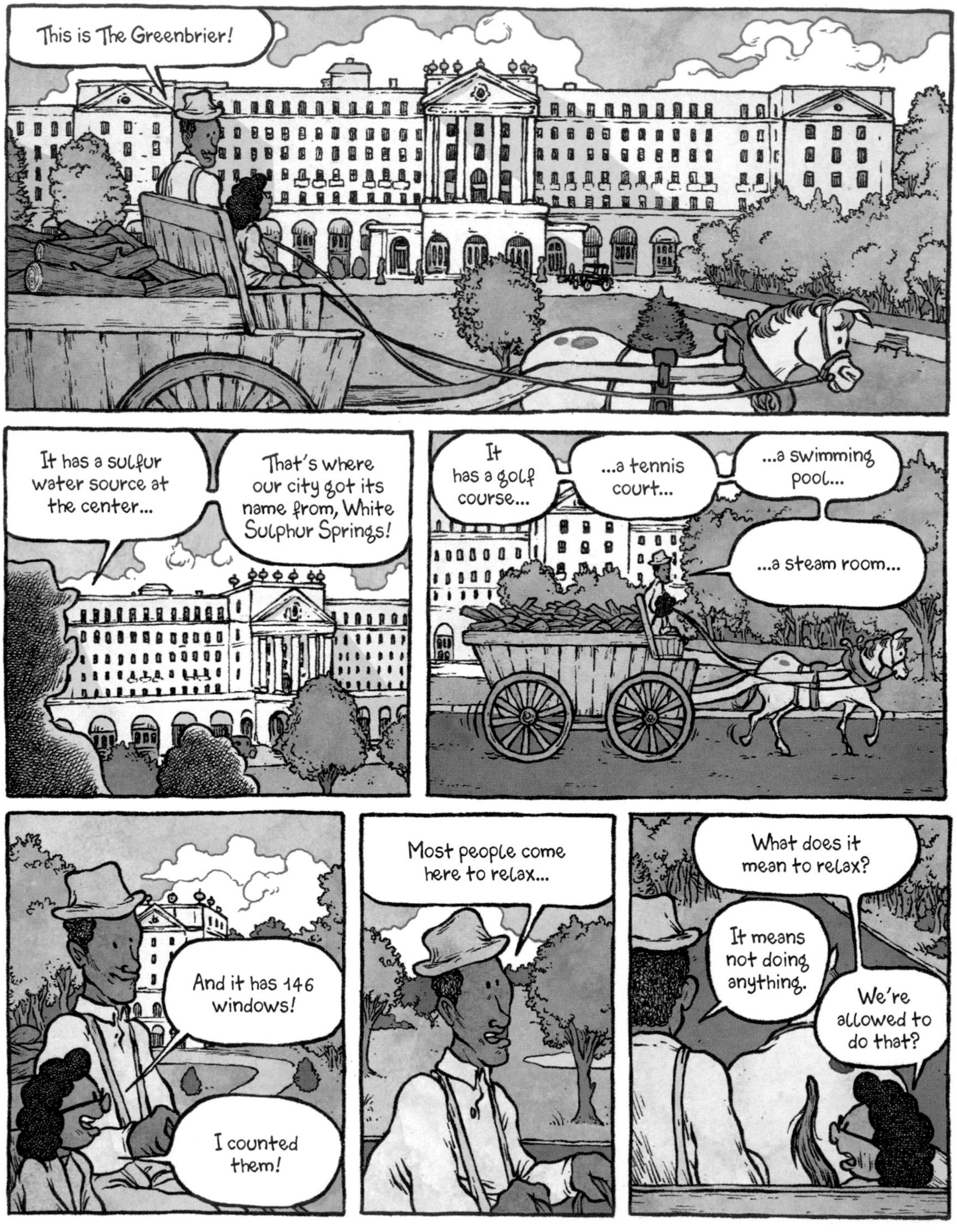
This is The Greenbrier!
It has a sulfur water source at the center...
That's where our city got its name from, White Sulphur Springs!
It has a golf course...
...a tennis court...
...a swimming pool...
...a steam room...
And it has 146 windows!
I counted them!
Most people come here to relax...
What does it mean to relax?
It means not doing anything.
We're allowed to do that?

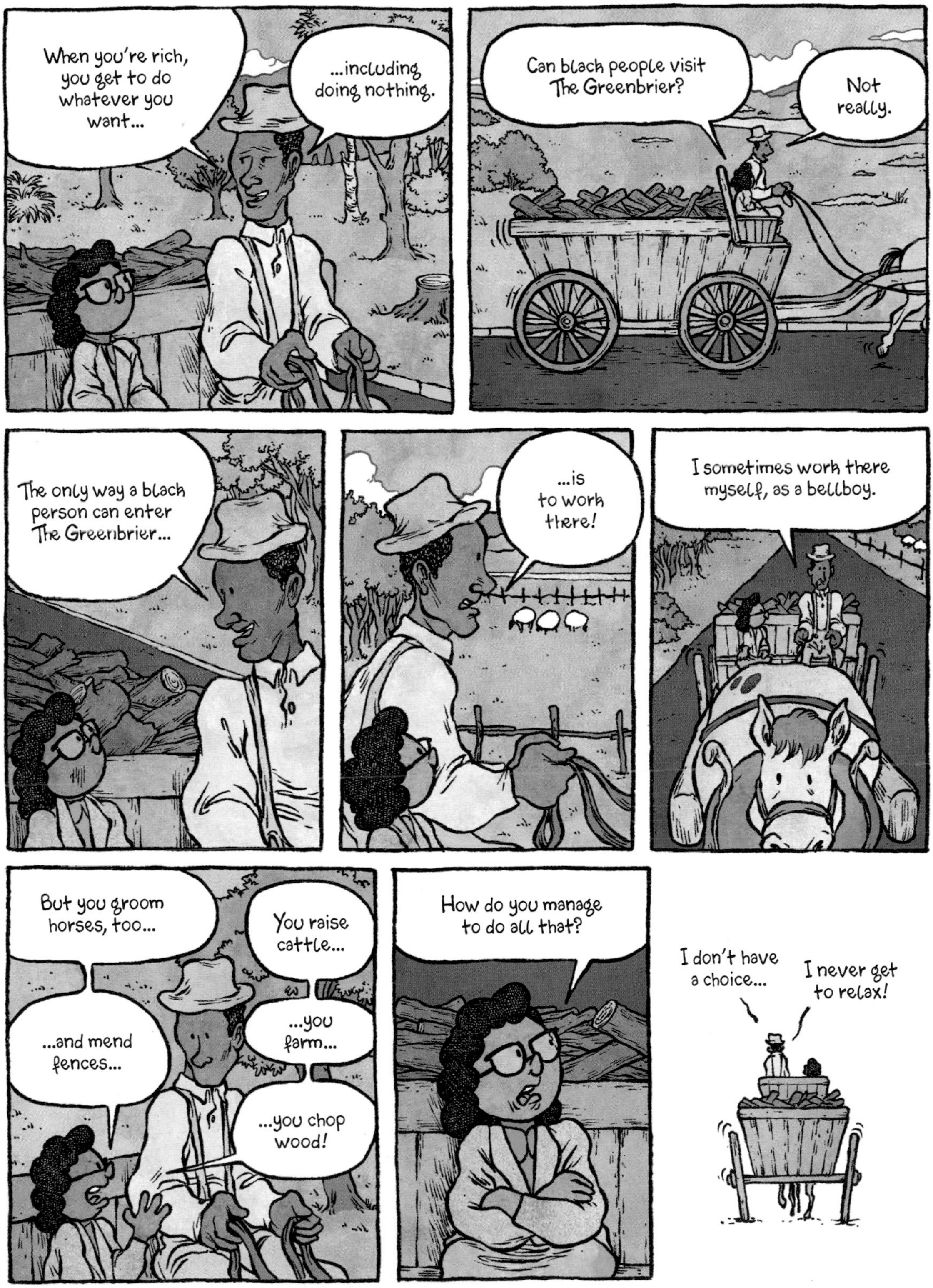
When you're rich, you get to do whatever you want...
...including doing nothing.
Can black people visit The Greenbrier?
Not really.
The only way a black person can enter The Greenbrier...
...is to work there!
I sometimes work there myself, as a bellboy.
But you groom horses, too...
You raise cattle...
...you farm...
...and mend fences...
...you chop wood!
How do you manage to do all that?
I don't have a choice...
I never get to relax!

X=Y

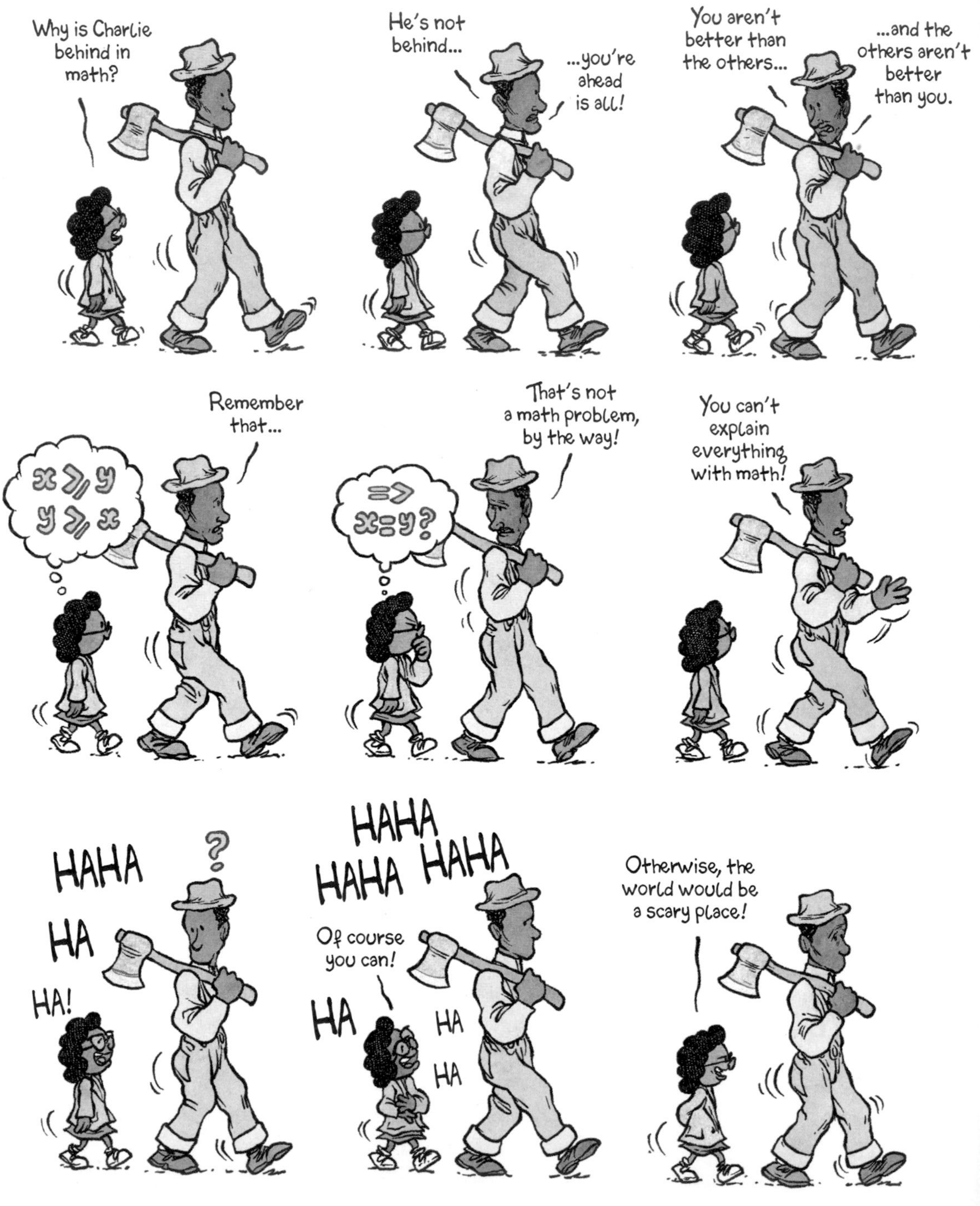

Why is Charlie behind in math?
He's not behind...
...you're ahead is all!
You aren't better than the others...
...and the others aren't better than you.
Remember that...
x ≥ y
y ≥ x
That's not a math problem, by the way!
=>
x=y?
You can't explain everything with math!
HAHA
?
HA
HA!
HAHA
HAHA HAHA
Of course you can!
HA
HA
HA
Otherwise, the world would be a scary place!

Cluck+Cluck=2

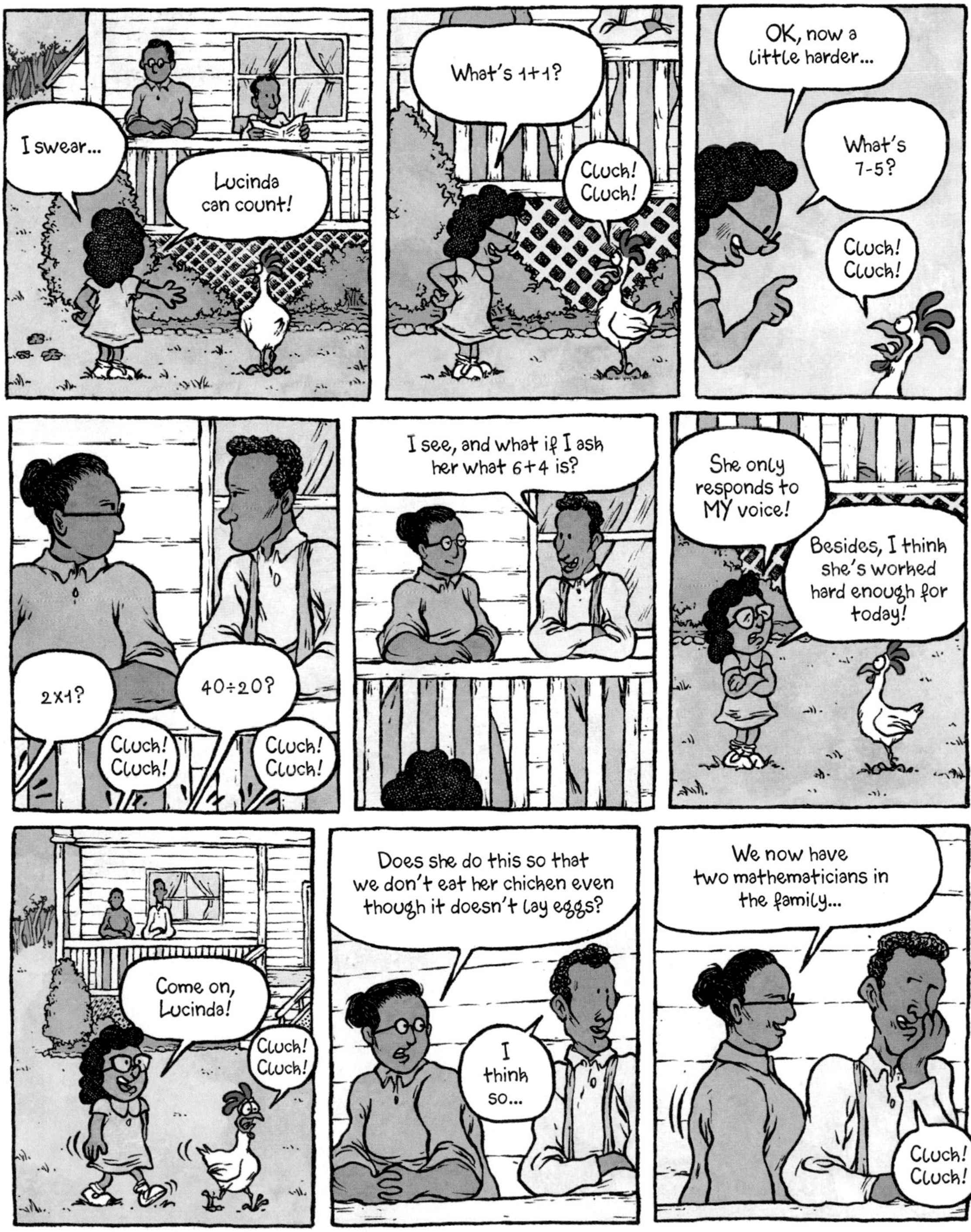
I swear...
Lucinda can count!
What's 1+1?
Cluck! Cluck!
OK, now a little harder...
What's 7-5?
Cluck! Cluck!
2x1?
Cluck! Cluck!
40÷20?
Cluck! Cluck!
I see, and what if I ask her what 6+4 is?
She only responds to MY voice!
Besides, I think she's worked hard enough for today!
Come on, Lucinda!
Cluck! Cluck!
Does she do this so that we don't eat her chicken even though it doesn't lay eggs?
I think so...
We now have two mathematicians in the family...
Cluck! Cluck!

Apollo 11

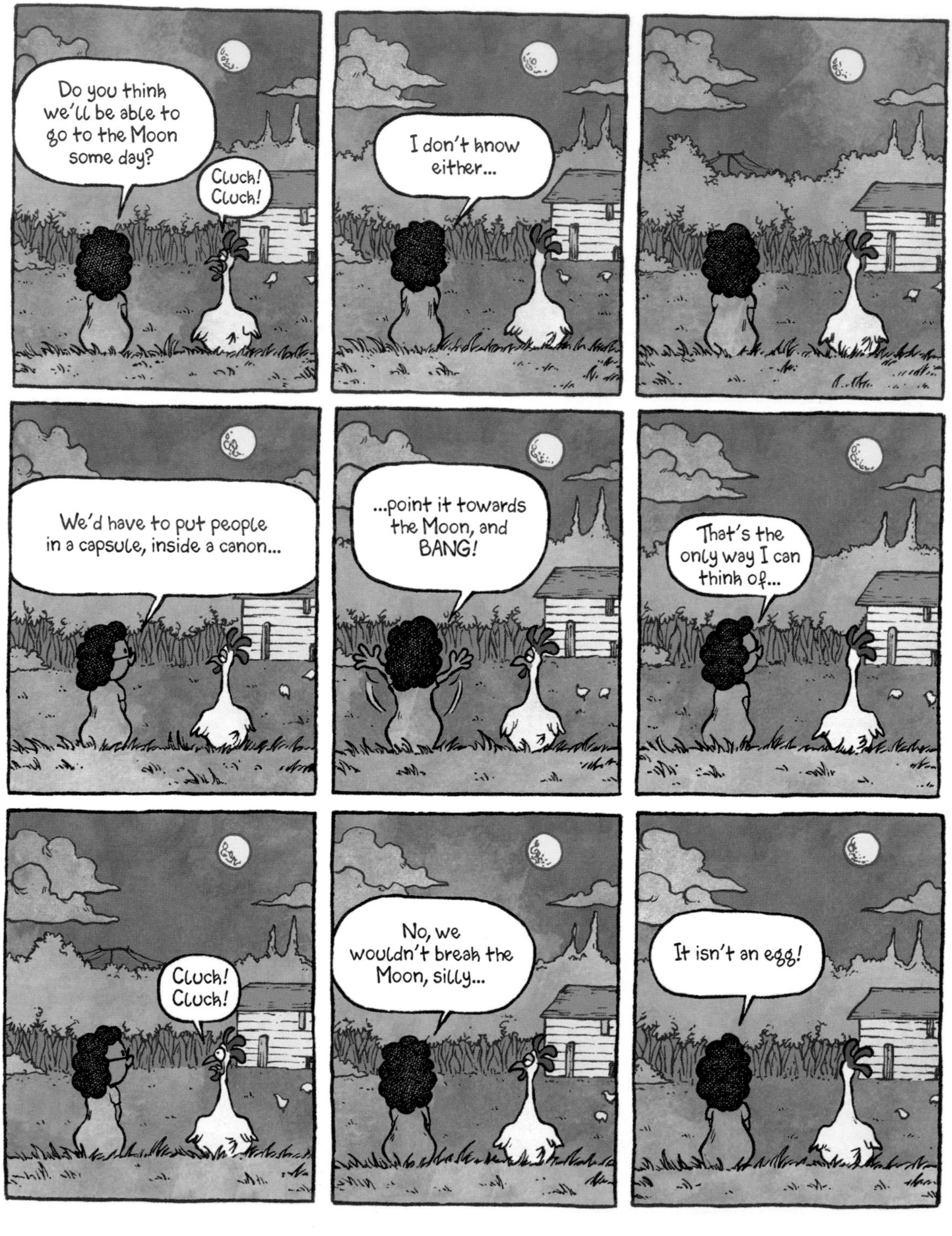
Do you think we'll be able to go to the Moon some day?
Cluck! Cluck!
I don't know either...
We'd have to put people in a capsule, inside a canon...
...point it towards the Moon, and BANG!
That's the only way I can think of...
Cluck! Cluck!
No, we wouldn't break the Moon, silly...
It isn't an egg!

H_2O=Skating Rink

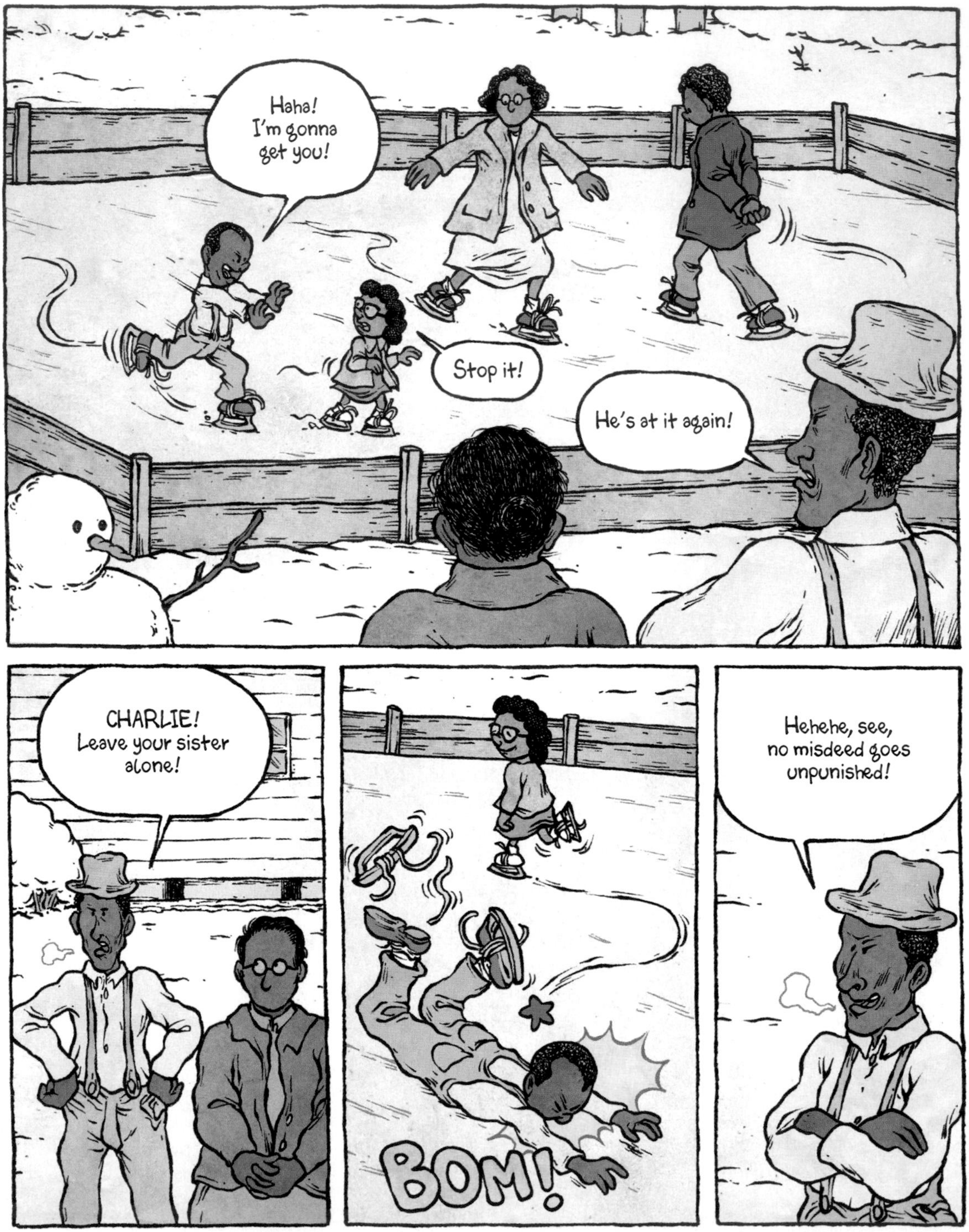
Haha! I'm gonna get you!
Stop it!
He's at it again!
CHARLIE! Leave your sister alone!
BOM!
Hehehe, see, no misdeed goes unpunished!

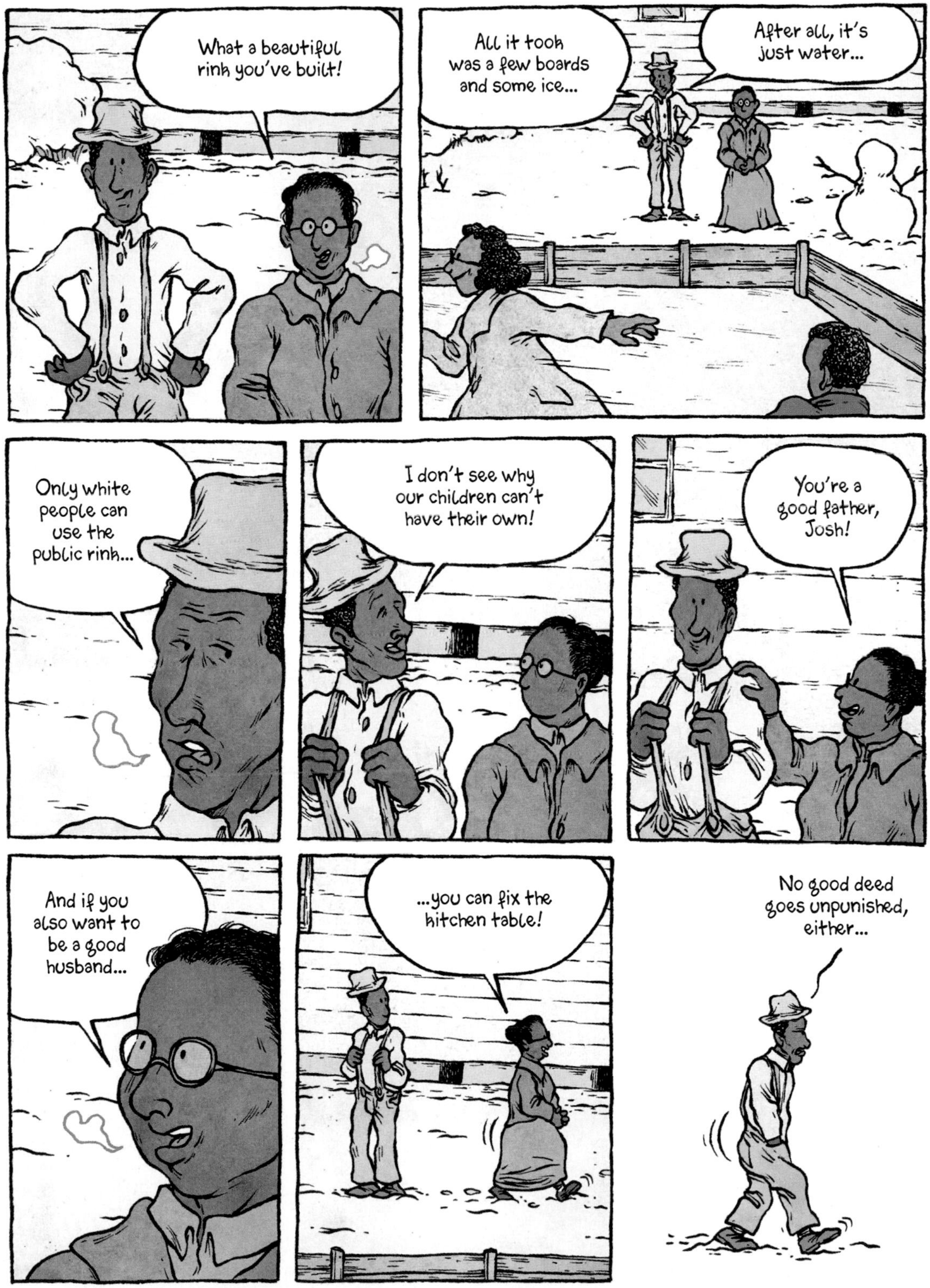
What a beautiful rink you've built!
All it took was a few boards and some ice...
After all, it's just water...
Only white people can use the public rink...
I don't see why our children can't have their own!
You're a good father, Josh!
And if you also want to be a good husband...
...you can fix the kitchen table!
No good deed goes unpunished, either...

A+B+C+D+E...=?

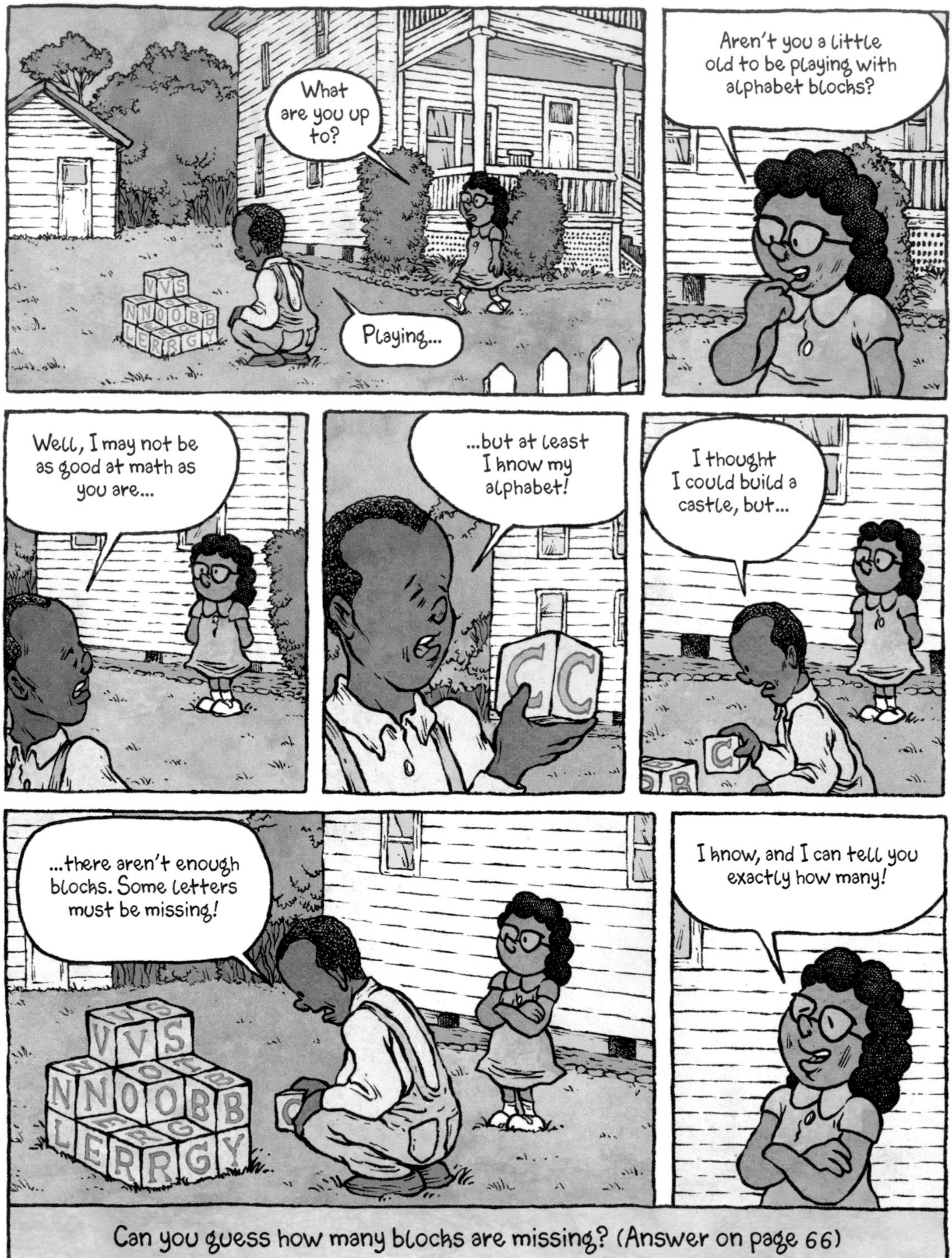
What are you up to?
Playing...
Aren't you a little old to be playing with alphabet blocks?
Well, I may not be as good at math as you are...
...but at least I know my alphabet!
I thought I could build a castle, but...
...there aren't enough blocks. Some letters must be missing!
I know, and I can tell you exactly how many!

Can you guess how many blocks are missing? (Answer on page 66)

1x Upon A Time

Sis, can you read me a story?

Sure. Cinderella, Little Red Riding Hood, or--

Nah, the same as usual!

I see, the 3rd grade math textbook...

Yeah, that one!

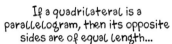

If a quadrilateral is a parallelogram, then its opposite sides are of equal length...

Seriously, Katherine, don't you want me to read you something a little more exciting?

It is exciting! If its diagonals are perpendicular and its 4 sides are of equal length...

...it's a rhombus!

And if its diagonals are the same length and its sides are perpendicular, it's a rectangle!

Oh, the suspense!

And if its a square, its a parallelogram, a rhombus, and a rectangle, all at once!

Are you telling the story or am I?

Keep going, but tell it with a spooky voice!

4.6

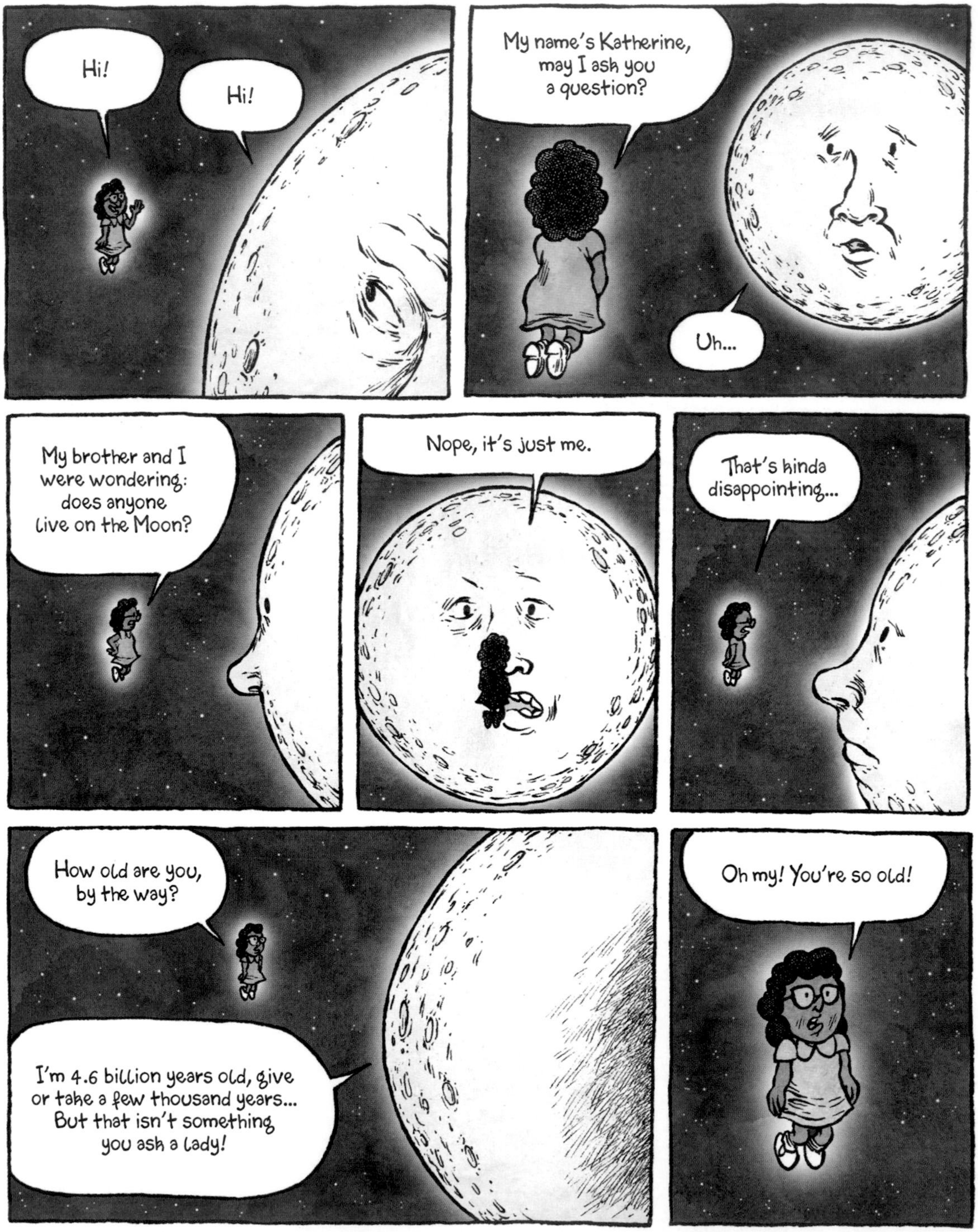
Hi!
Hi!
My name's Katherine, may I ask you a question?
Uh...
My brother and I were wondering: does anyone live on the Moon?
Nope, it's just me.
That's kinda disappointing...
How old are you, by the way?
I'm 4.6 billion years old, give or take a few thousand years... But that isn't something you ask a lady!
Oh my! You're so old!

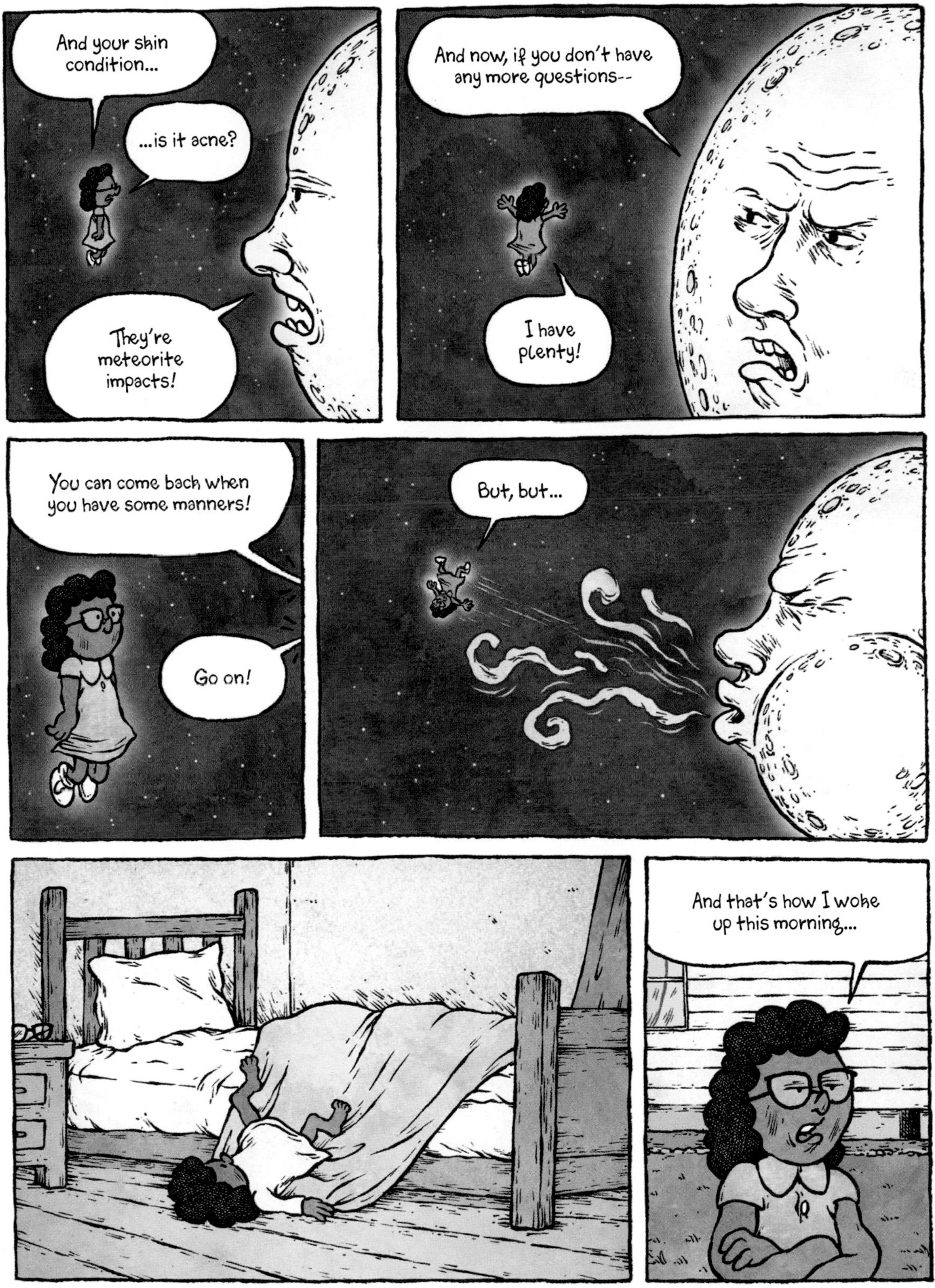

And your skin condition...
...is it acne?
They're meteorite impacts!
And now, if you don't have any more questions--
I have plenty!
You can come back when you have some manners!
Go on!
But, but...
And that's how I woke up this morning...

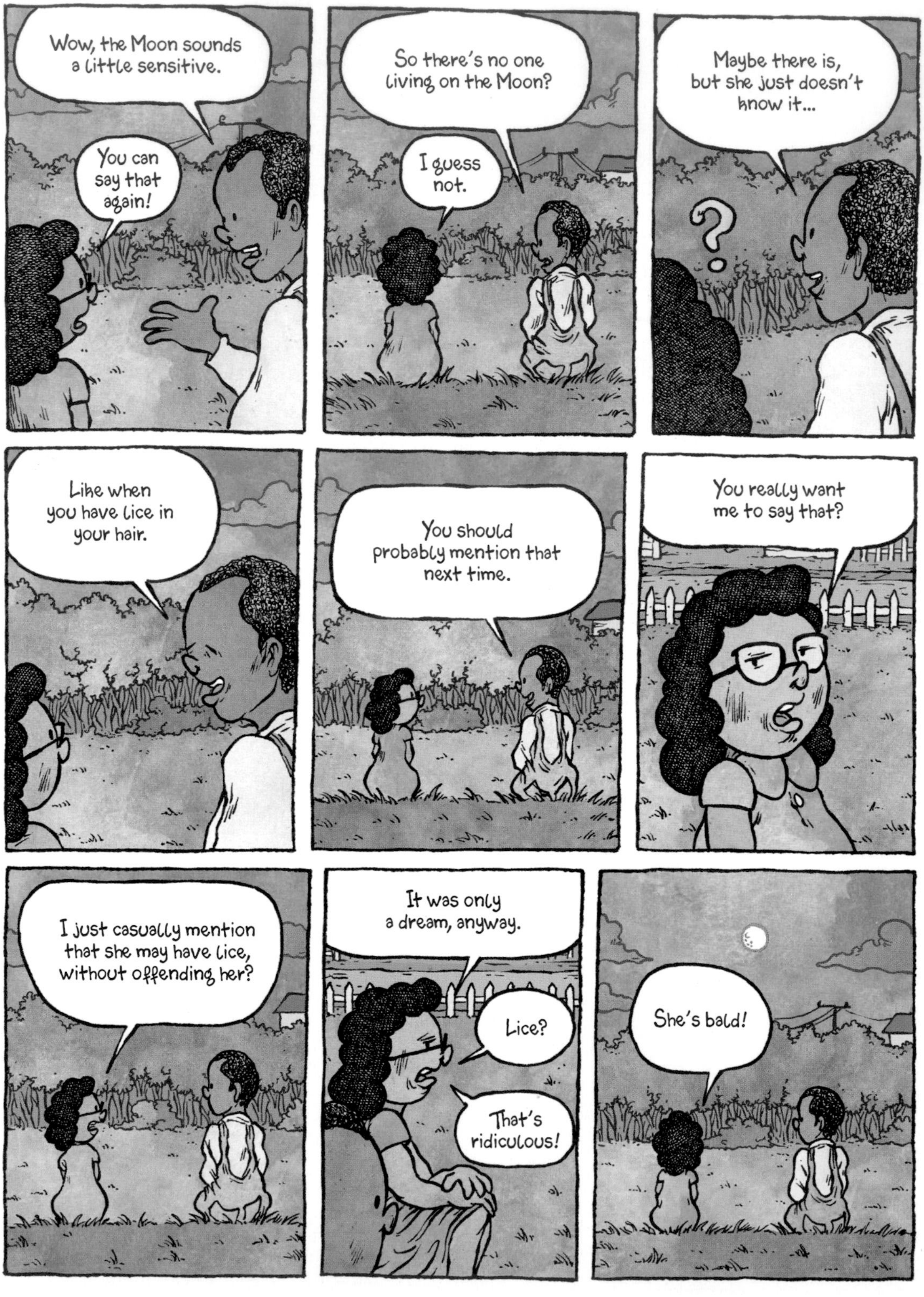
Wow, the Moon sounds a little sensitive.
You can say that again!
So there's no one living on the Moon?
I guess not.
Maybe there is, but she just doesn't know it...
?
Like when you have lice in your hair.
You should probably mention that next time.
You really want me to say that?
I just casually mention that she may have lice, without offending her?
It was only a dream, anyway.
Lice?
That's ridiculous!
She's bald!

57

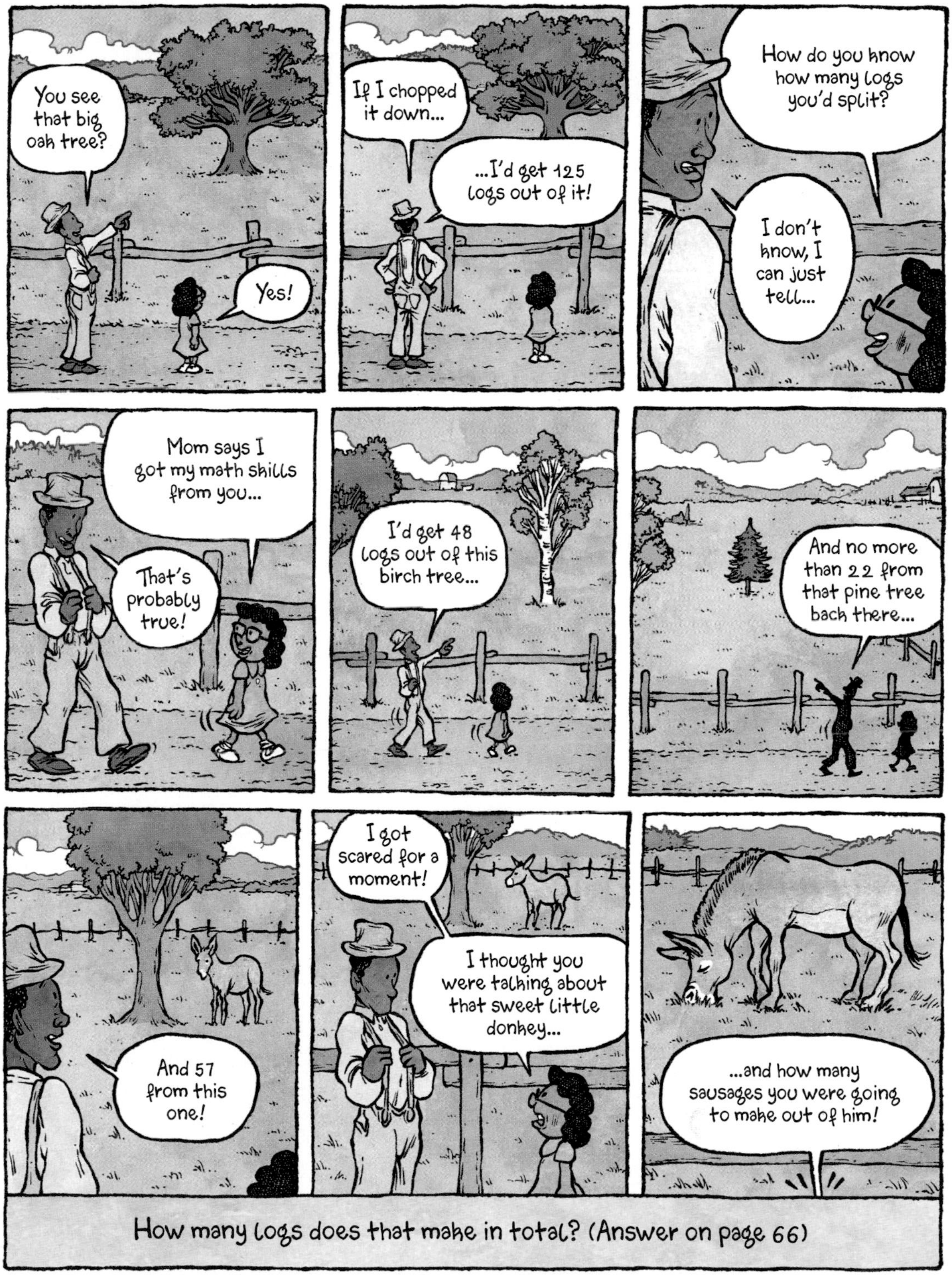
You see that big oak tree?
Yes!
If I chopped it down...
...I'd get 125 logs out of it!
How do you know how many logs you'd split?
I don't know, I can just tell...
Mom says I got my math skills from you...
That's probably true!
I'd get 48 logs out of this birch tree...
And no more than 22 from that pine tree back there...
And 57 from this one!
I got scared for a moment!
I thought you were talking about that sweet little donkey...
...and how many sausages you were going to make out of him!

How many logs does that make in total? (Answer on page 66)

≤

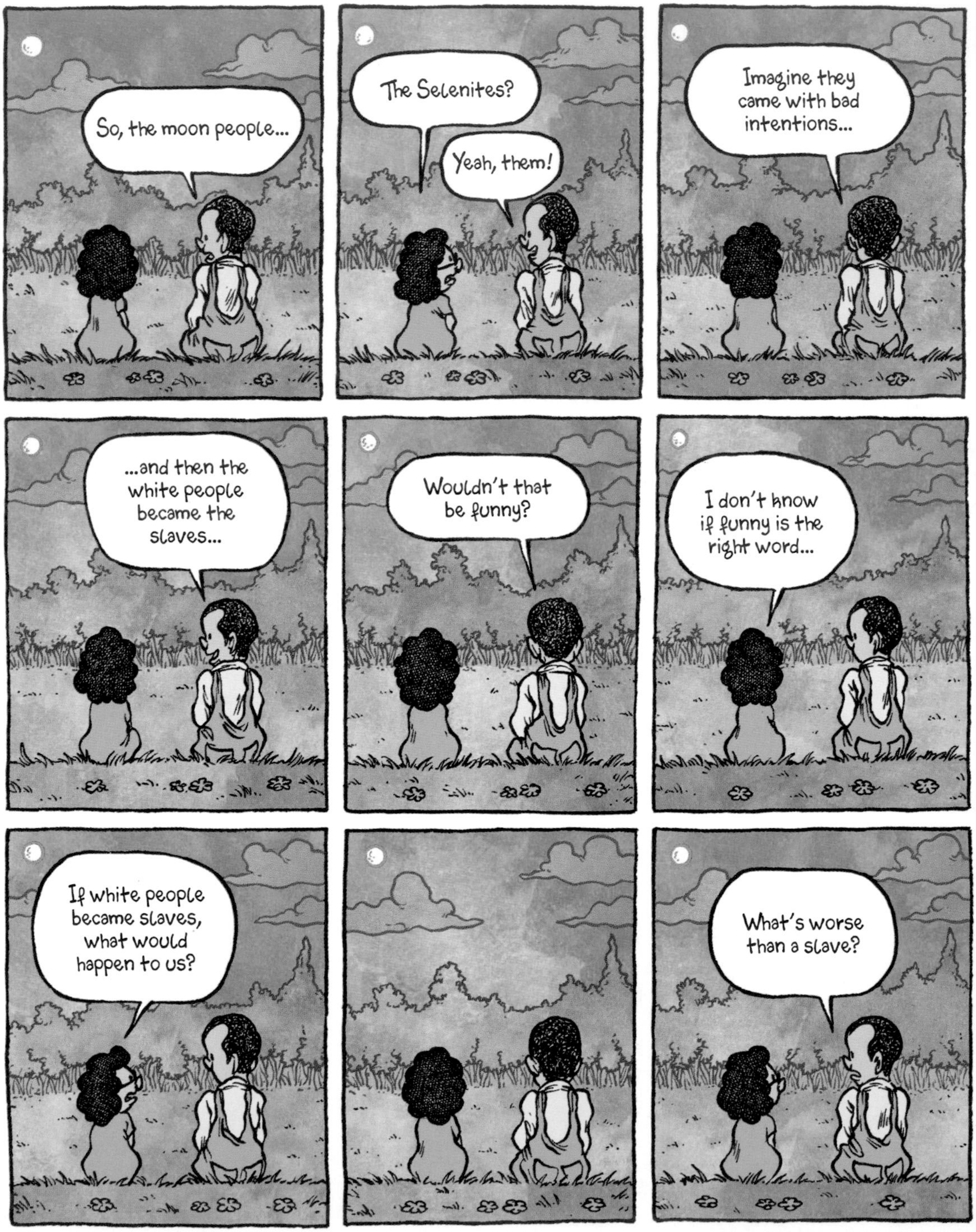
So, the moon people...
The Selenites?
Yeah, them!
Imagine they came with bad intentions...
...and then the white people became the slaves...
Wouldn't that be funny?
I don't know if funny is the right word...
If white people became slaves, what would happen to us?
What's worse than a slave?

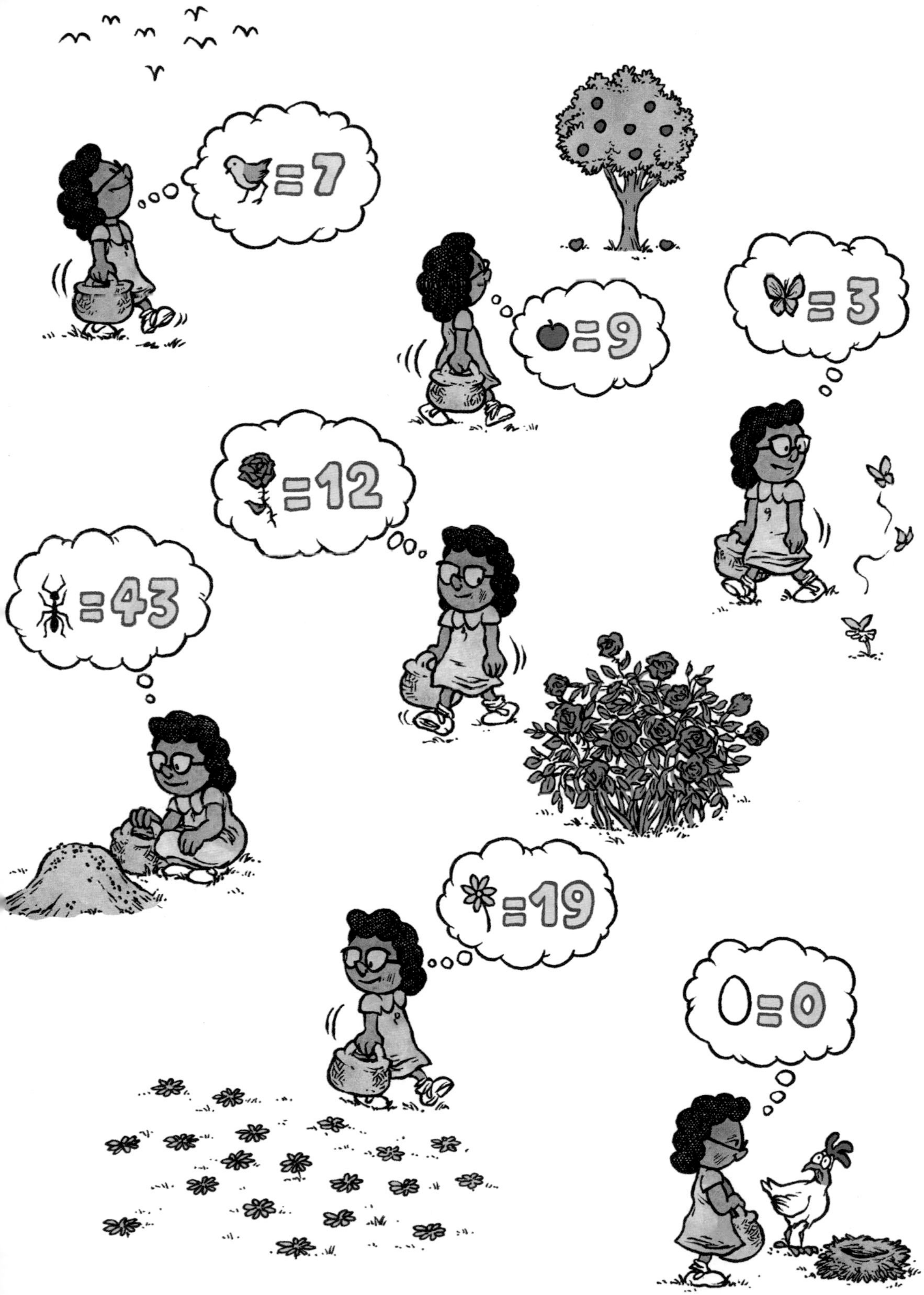
=7
=9
=3
=12
=43
=19
=0

7

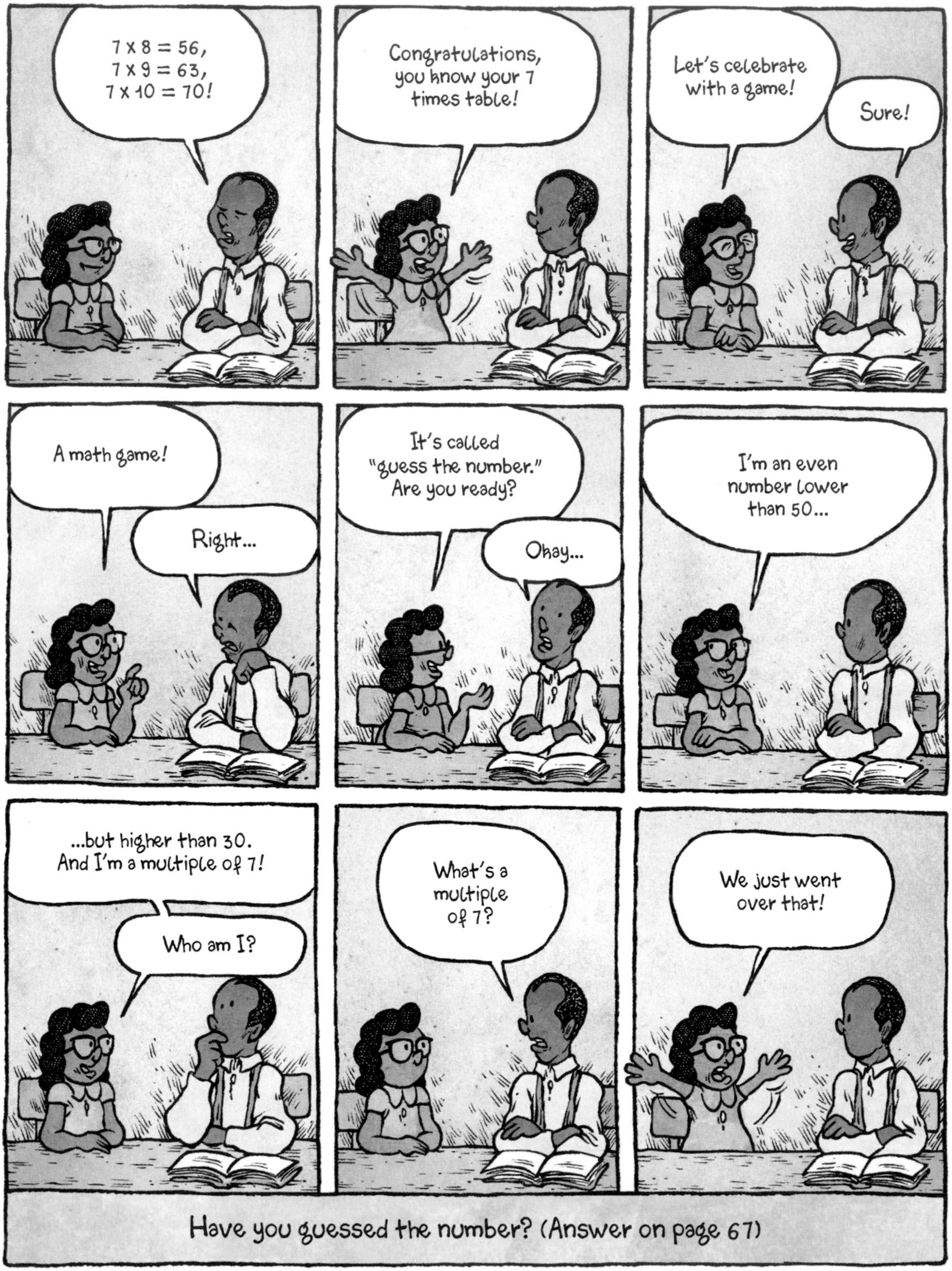
7 x 8 = 56,
7 x 9 = 63,
7 x 10 = 70!
Congratulations, you know your 7 times table!
Let's celebrate with a game!
Sure!
A math game!
Right...
It's called "guess the number." Are you ready?
Okay...
I'm an even number lower than 50...
...but higher than 30. And I'm a multiple of 7!
Who am I?
What's a multiple of 7?
We just went over that!
Have you guessed the number? (Answer on page 67)

Pepper = $C_{17}H_{19}NO_3$

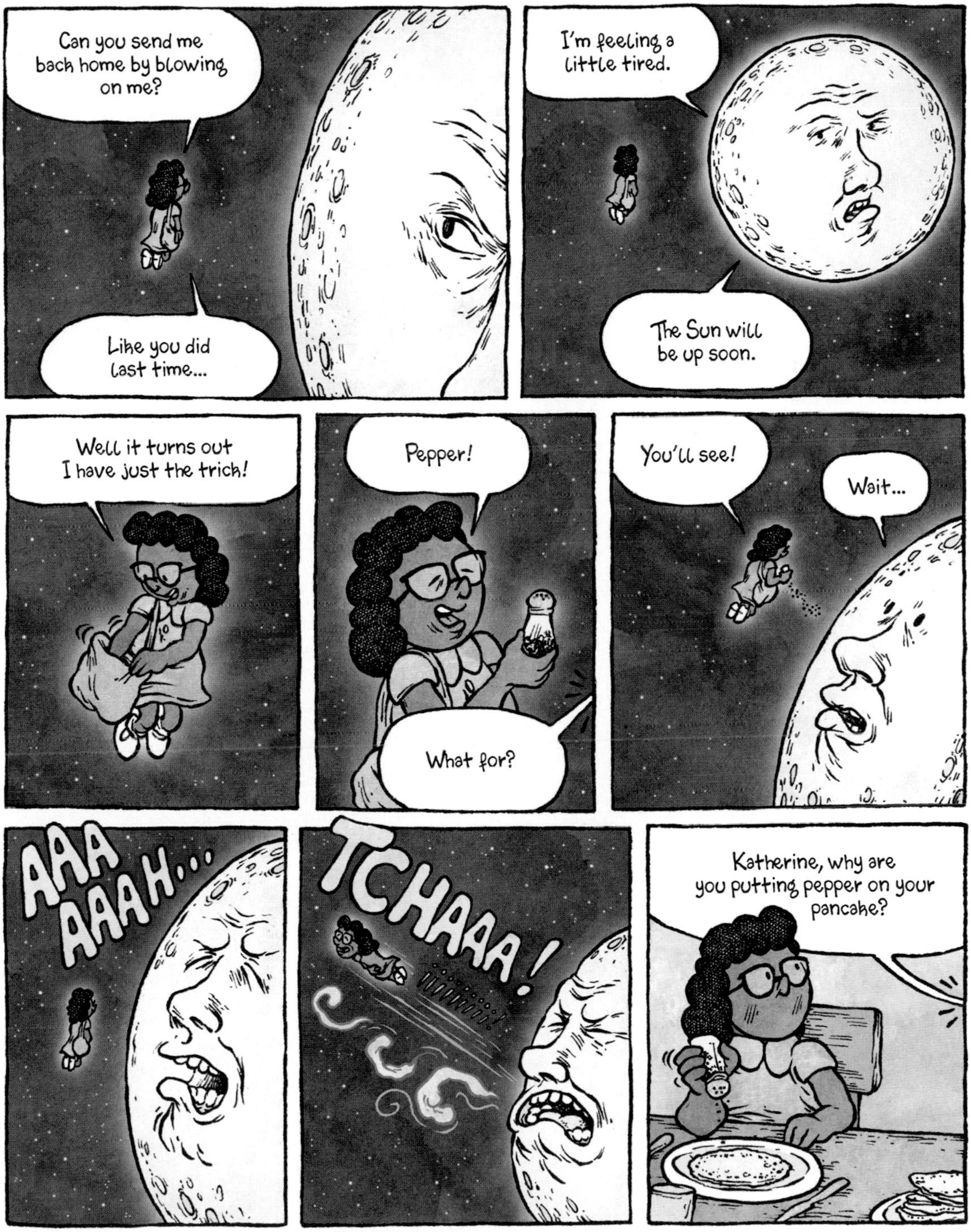

Can you send me back home by blowing on me?
Like you did last time...
I'm feeling a little tired.
The Sun will be up soon.
Well it turns out I have just the trick!
Pepper!
What for?
You'll see!
Wait...
AAA AAAH...
TCHAAA!
Katherine, why are you putting pepper on your pancake?

238,855 Miles

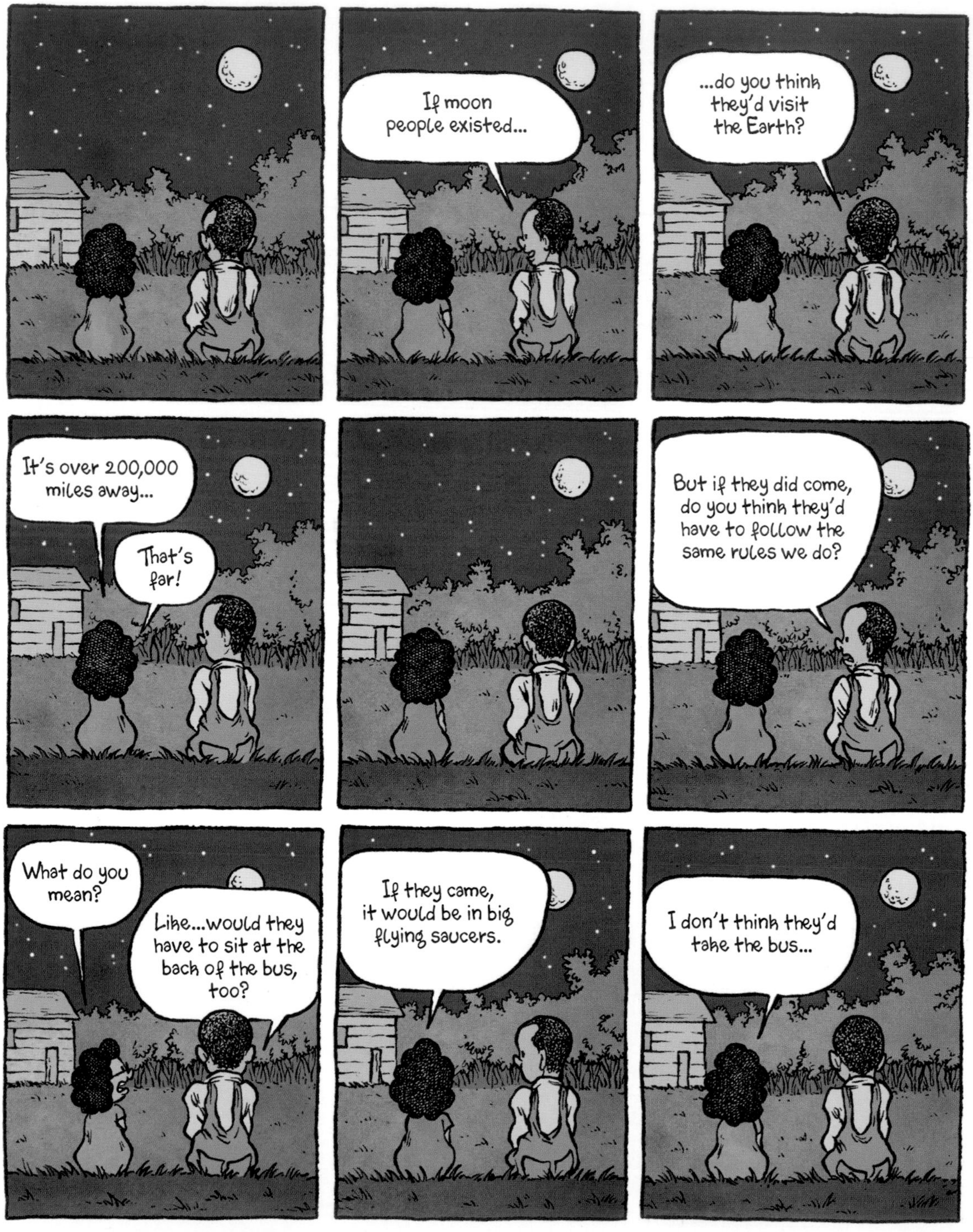

If moon people existed...
...do you think they'd visit the Earth?
It's over 200,000 miles away...
That's far!
But if they did come, do you think they'd have to follow the same rules we do?
What do you mean?
Like...would they have to sit at the back of the bus, too?
If they came, it would be in big flying saucers.
I don't think they'd take the bus...

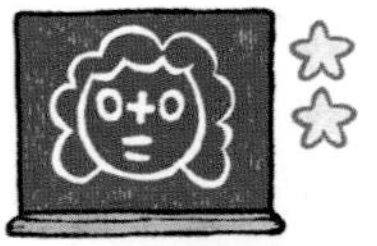

1

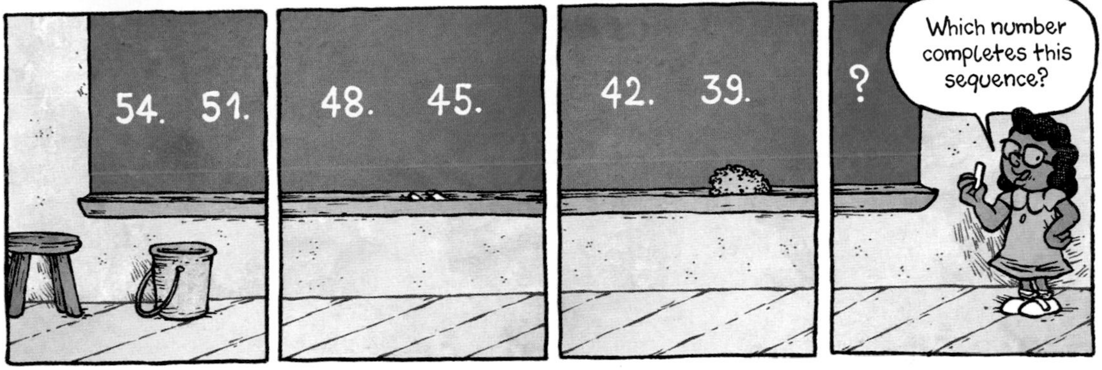
54. 51.
48. 45.
42. 39.
?
Which number completes this sequence?

2

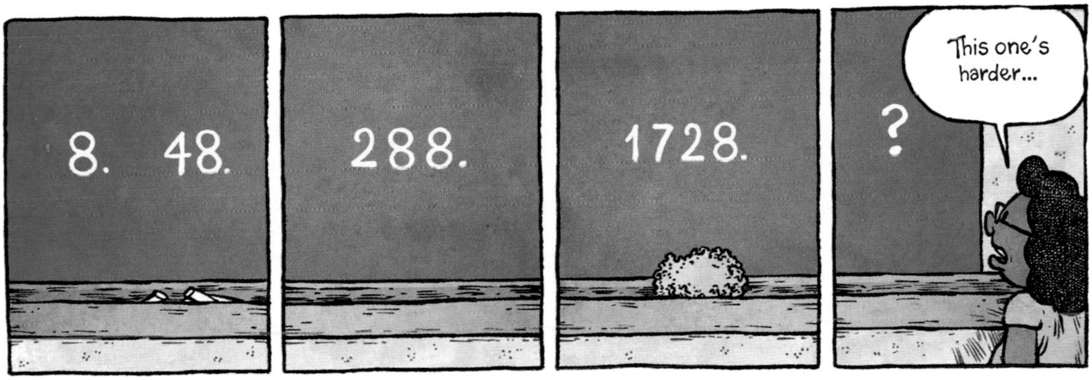
8. 48.
288.
1728.
?
This one's harder...

3

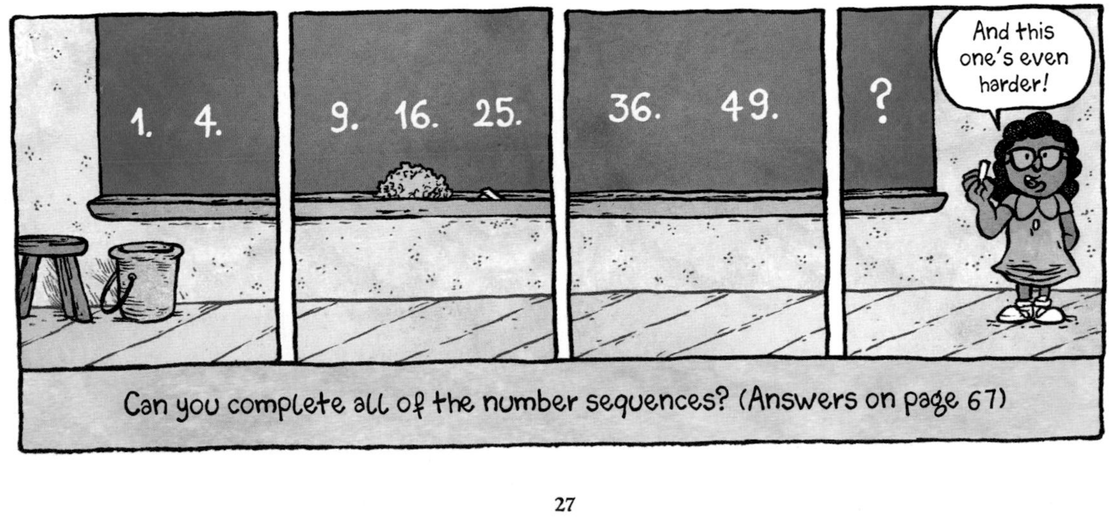
1. 4.
9. 16. 25.
36. 49.
?
And this one's even harder!

Can you complete all of the number sequences? (Answers on page 67)

H_2O

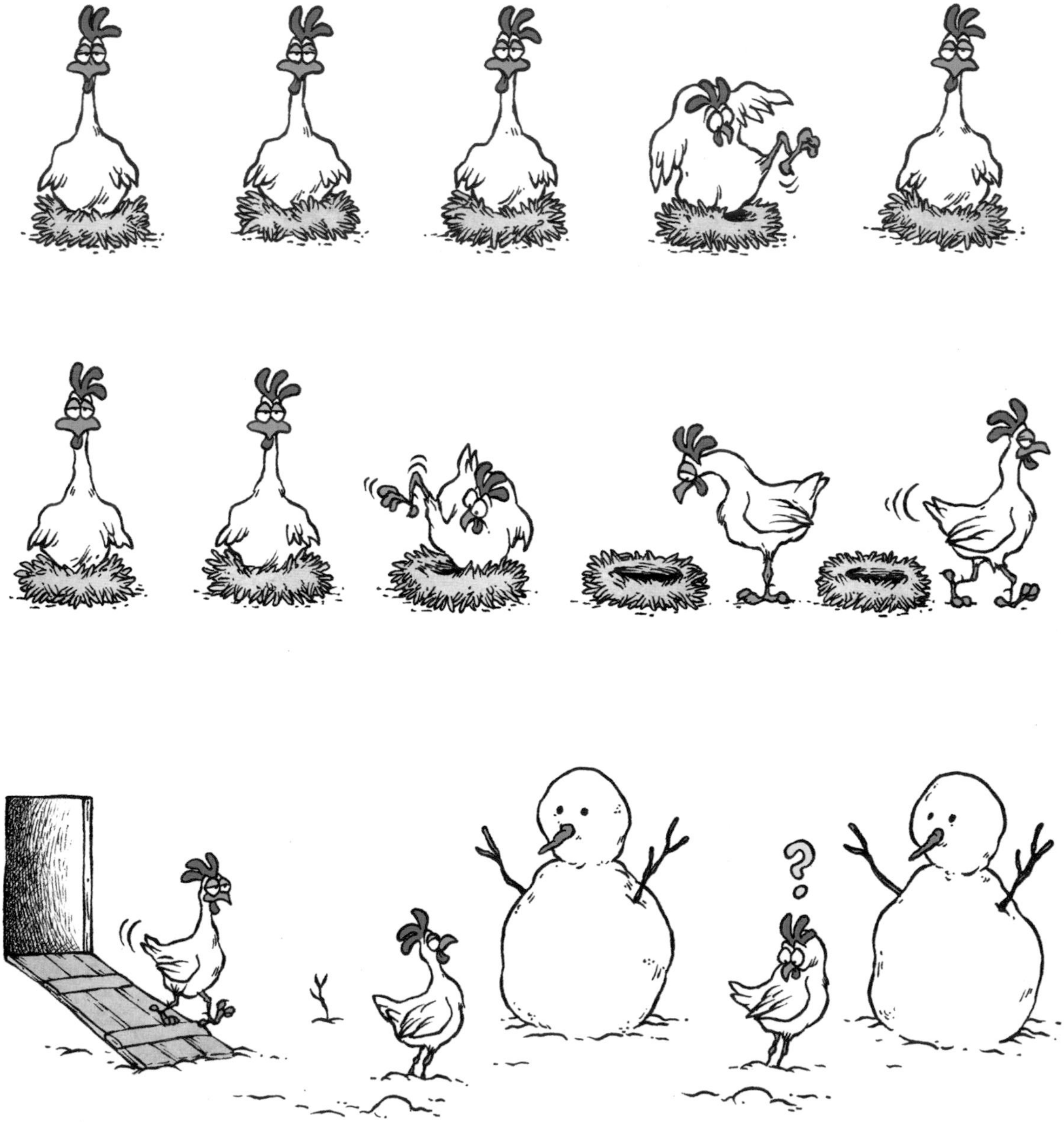

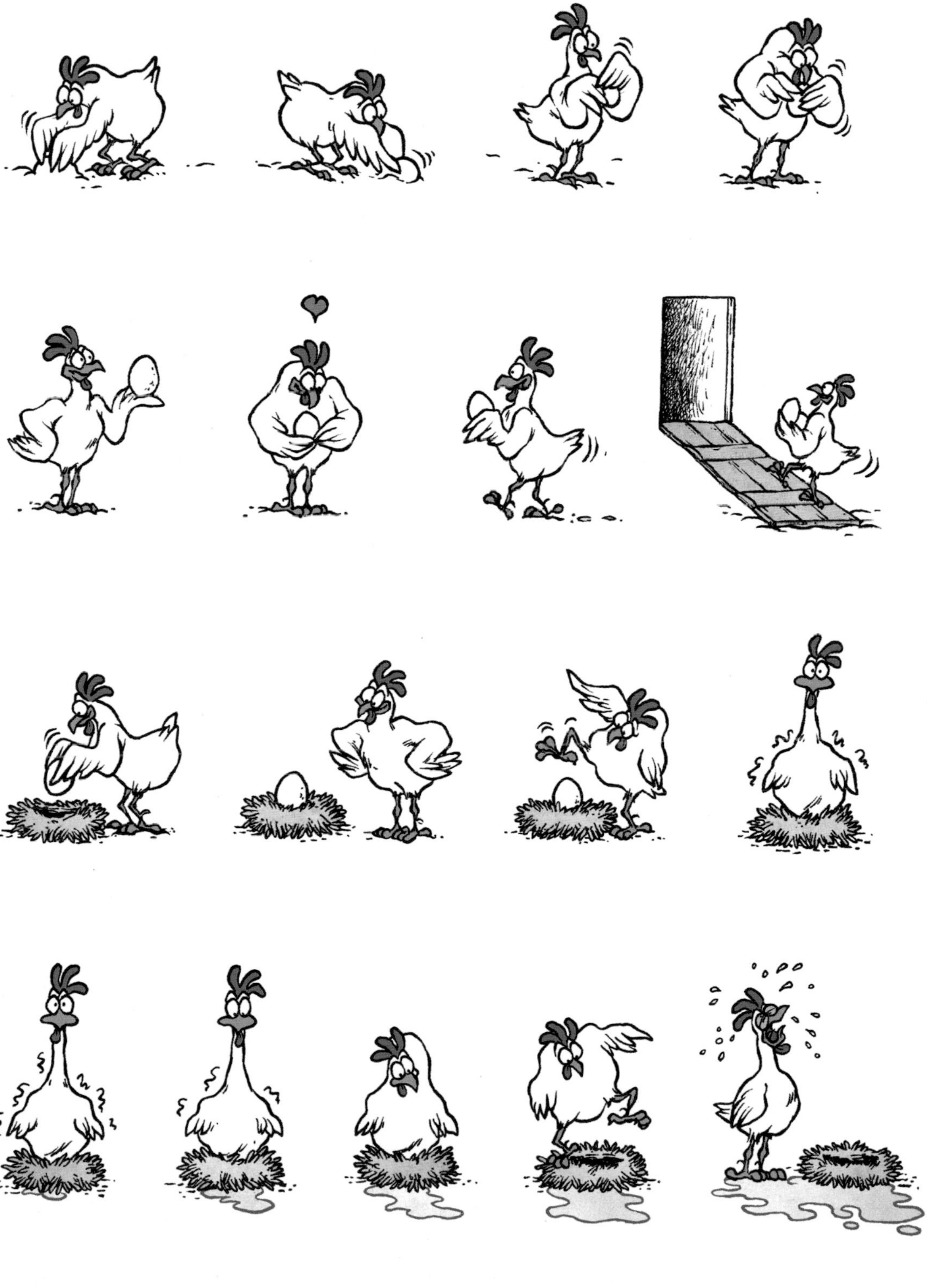

200,000,000,000

How many stars are there in the galaxy?

Between 200 and 400 billion!

That's a lot...

Did you know that when you look at a star, you're actually looking into the past?

What do you mean?

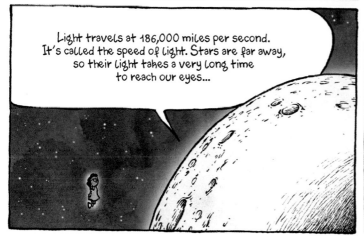

Light travels at 186,000 miles per second. It's called the speed of light. Stars are far away, so their light takes a very long time to reach our eyes...

When you look at a star that's 1,000 light years away from Earth, you see it as it was 1,000 years ago!

Oooh...

I'll remember that next time I count the stars...

You'll probably be counting them sooner than you think.

What do you mean?

180

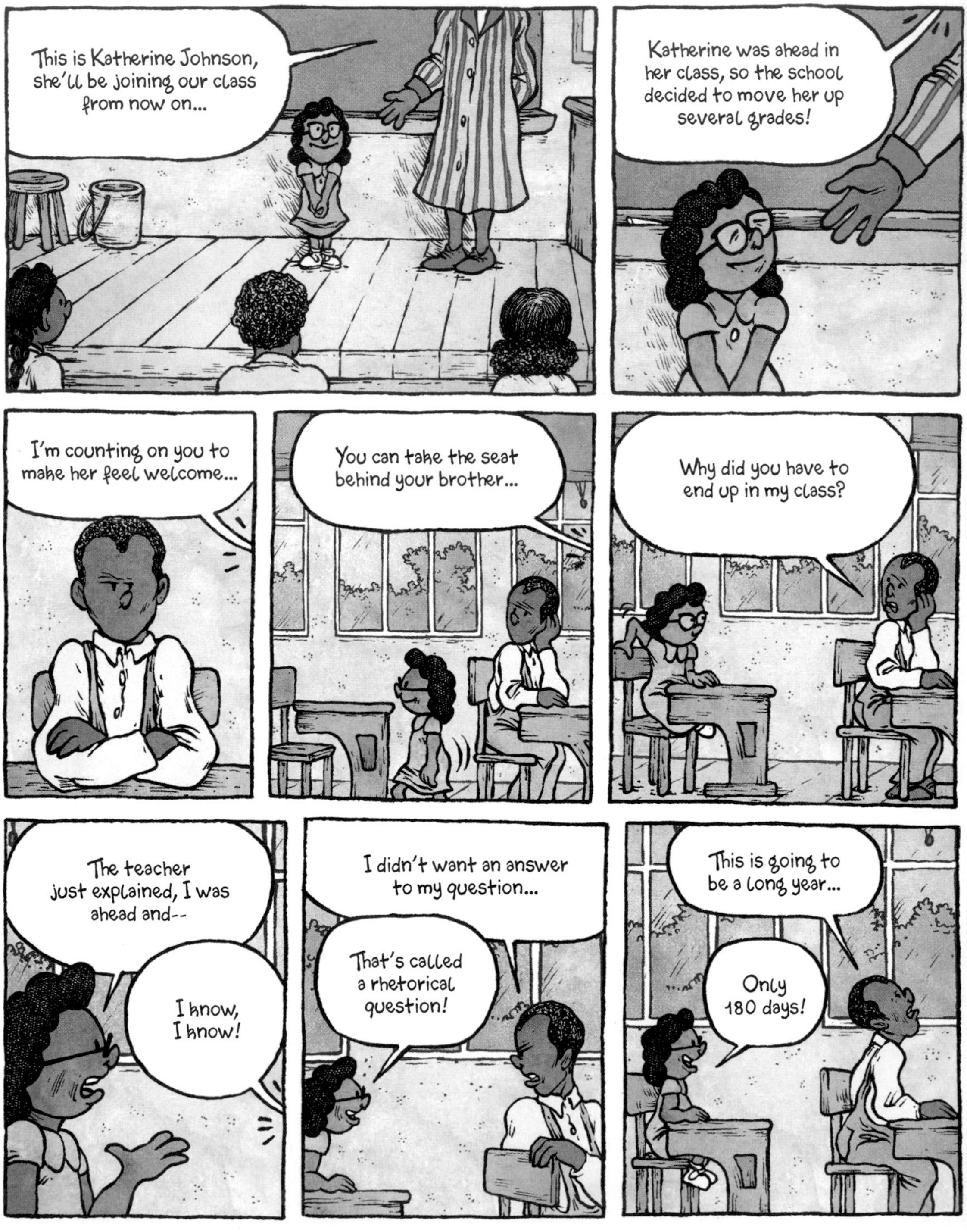
This is Katherine Johnson, she'll be joining our class from now on...
Katherine was ahead in her class, so the school decided to move her up several grades!
I'm counting on you to make her feel welcome...
You can take the seat behind your brother...
Why did you have to end up in my class?
The teacher just explained, I was ahead and--
I know, I know!
I didn't want an answer to my question...
That's called a rhetorical question!
This is going to be a long year...
Only 180 days!

x5

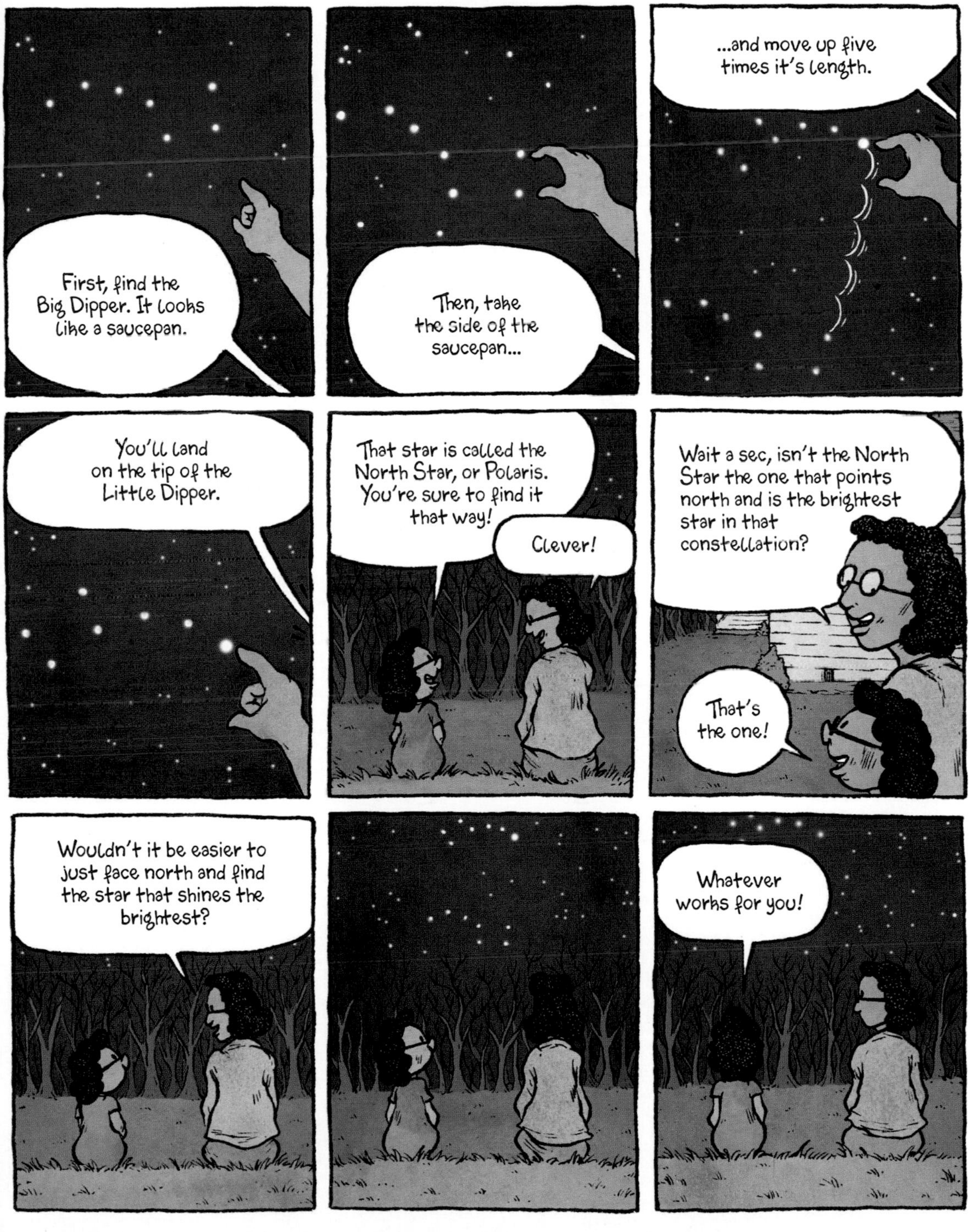
First, find the Big Dipper. It looks like a saucepan.
Then, take the side of the saucepan...
...and move up five times it's length.
You'll land on the tip of the Little Dipper.
That star is called the North Star, or Polaris. You're sure to find it that way!
Clever!
Wait a sec, isn't the North Star the one that points north and is the brightest star in that constellation?
That's the one!
Wouldn't it be easier to just face north and find the star that shines the brightest?
Whatever works for you!

48,000

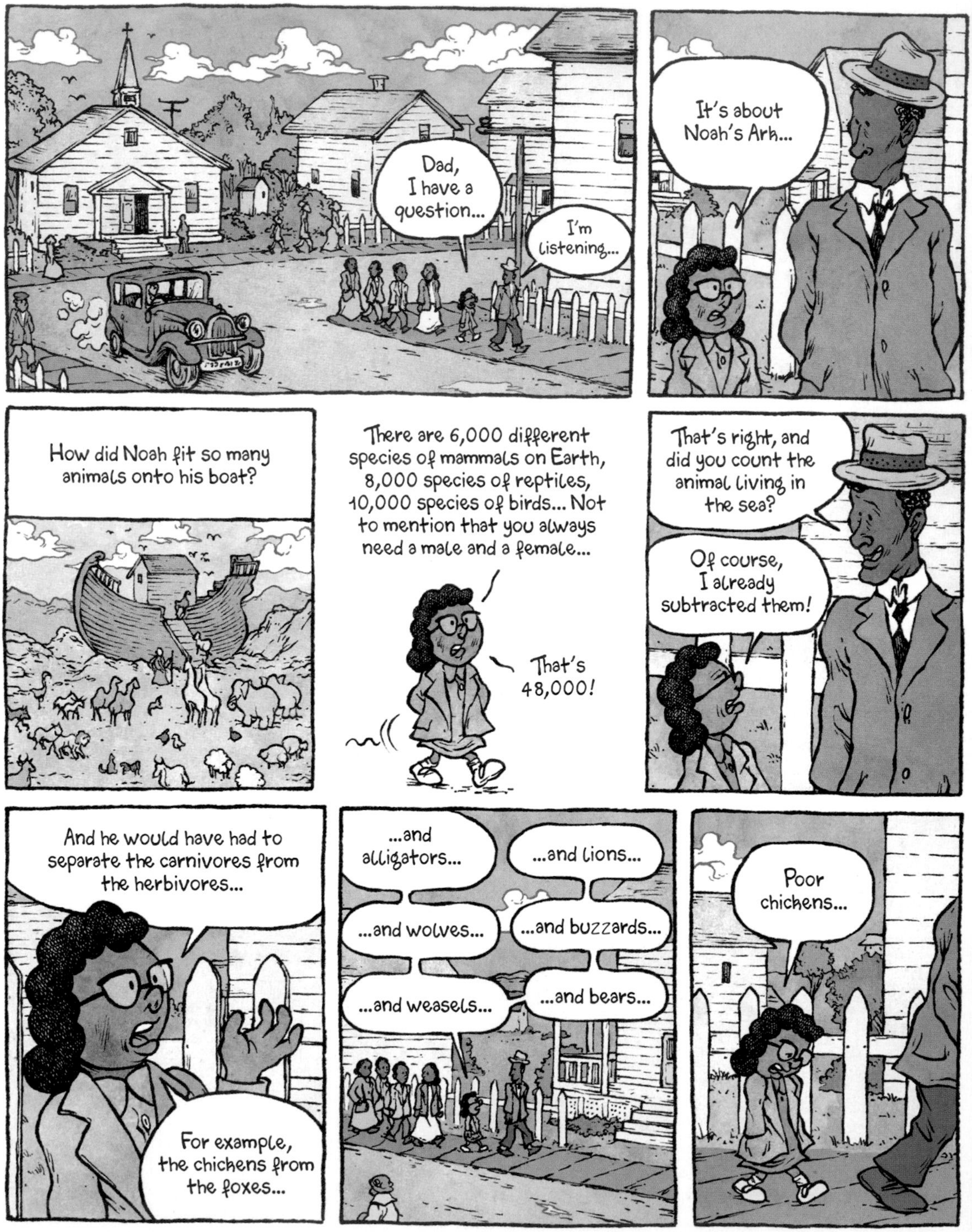
Dad, I have a question...
I'm listening...
It's about Noah's Ark...
How did Noah fit so many animals onto his boat?
There are 6,000 different species of mammals on Earth, 8,000 species of reptiles, 10,000 species of birds... Not to mention that you always need a male and a female...
That's 48,000!
That's right, and did you count the animal living in the sea?
Of course, I already subtracted them!
And he would have had to separate the carnivores from the herbivores...
For example, the chickens from the foxes...
...and alligators...
...and lions...
...and wolves...
...and buzzards...
...and weasels...
...and bears...
Poor chickens...

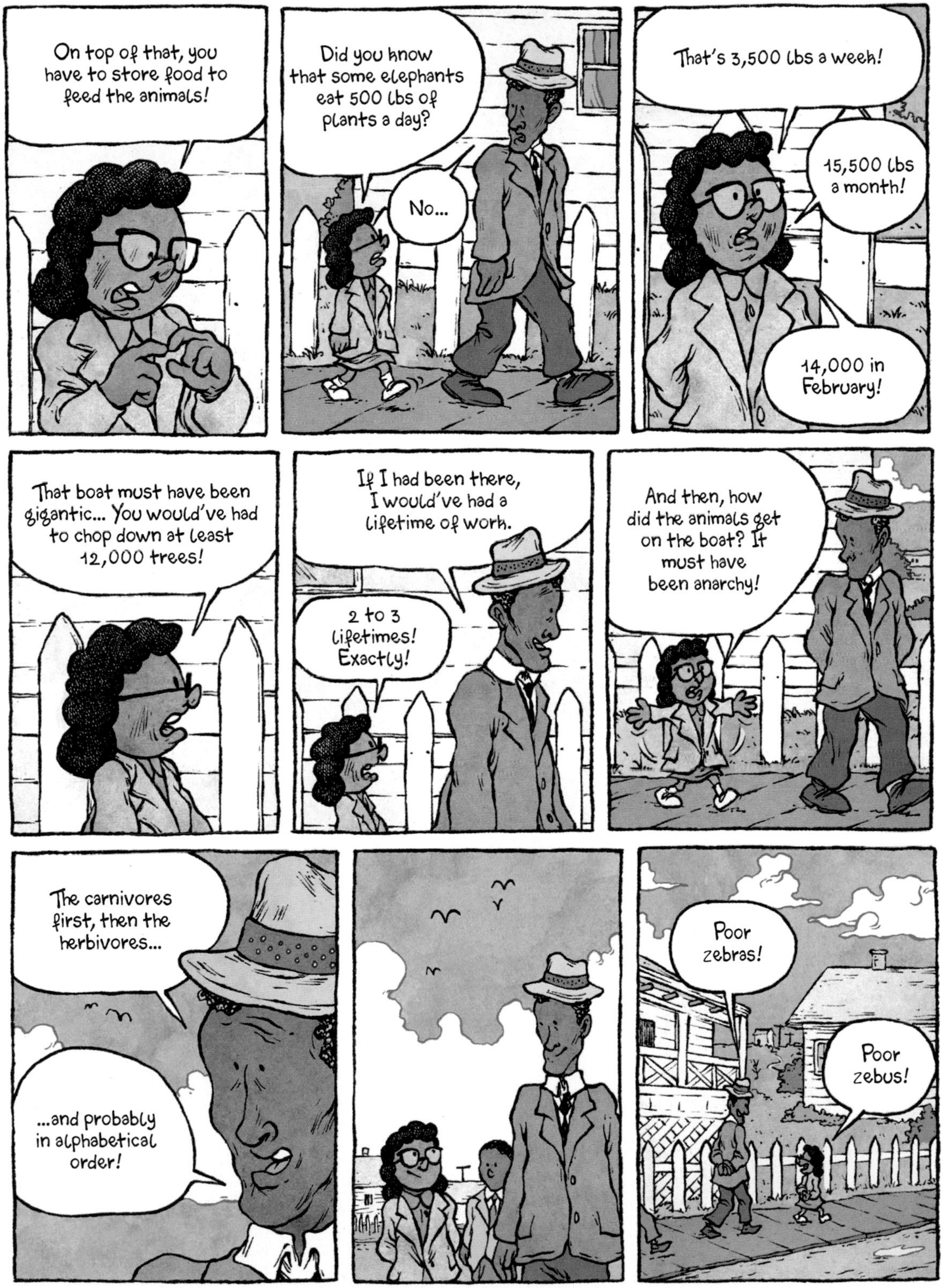

On top of that, you have to store food to feed the animals!
Did you know that some elephants eat 500 lbs of plants a day?
No...
That's 3,500 lbs a week!
15,500 lbs a month!
14,000 in February!
That boat must have been gigantic... You would've had to chop down at least 12,000 trees!
If I had been there, I would've had a lifetime of work.
2 to 3 lifetimes! Exactly!
And then, how did the animals get on the boat? It must have been anarchy!
The carnivores first, then the herbivores...
...and probably in alphabetical order!
Poor zebras!
Poor zebus!

4

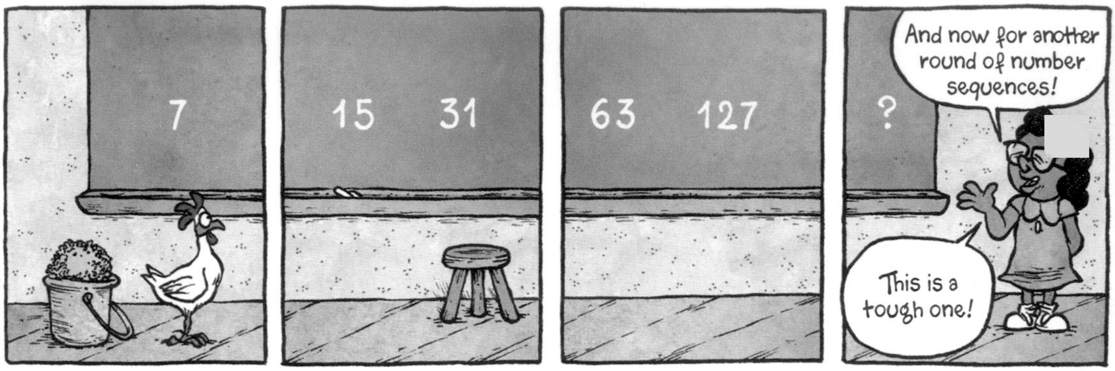
7
15 31
63 127
?
And now for another round of number sequences!
This is a tough one!

5

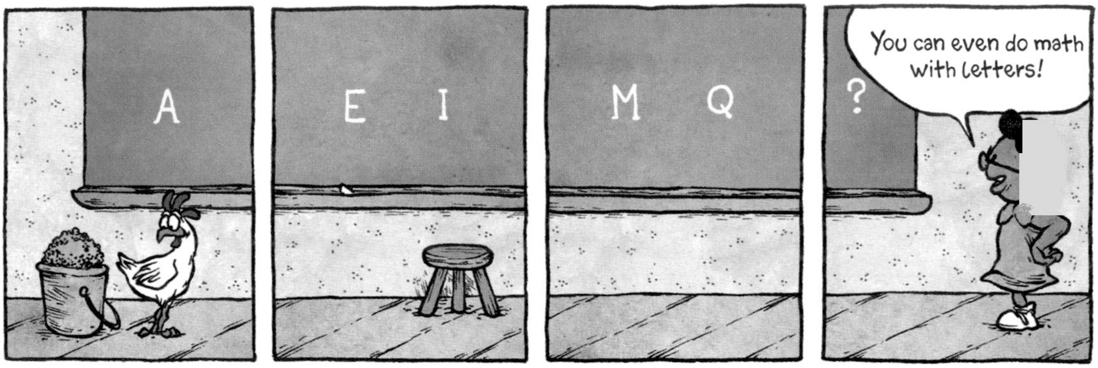
A
E I
M Q
?
You can even do math with letters!

6

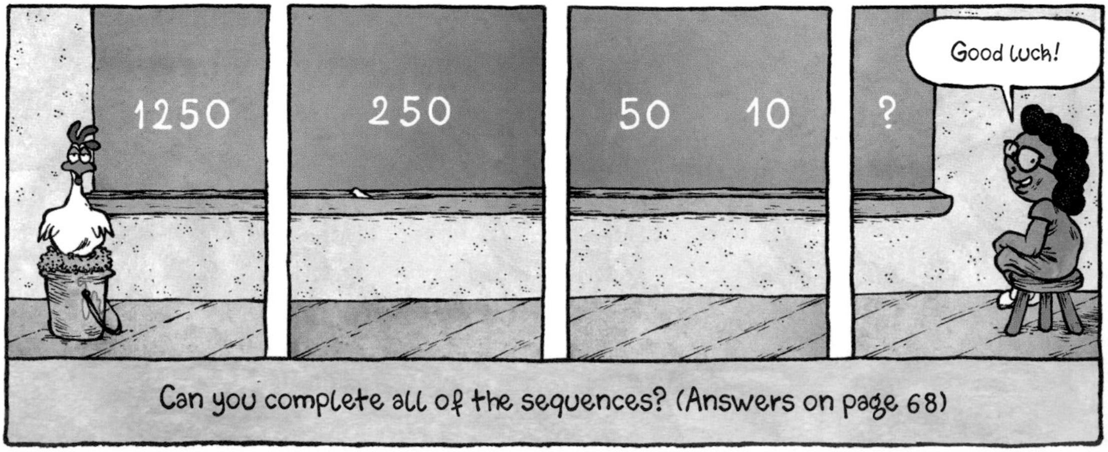
1250
250
50 10
?
Good luck!
Can you complete all of the sequences? (Answers on page 68)

1+1=?

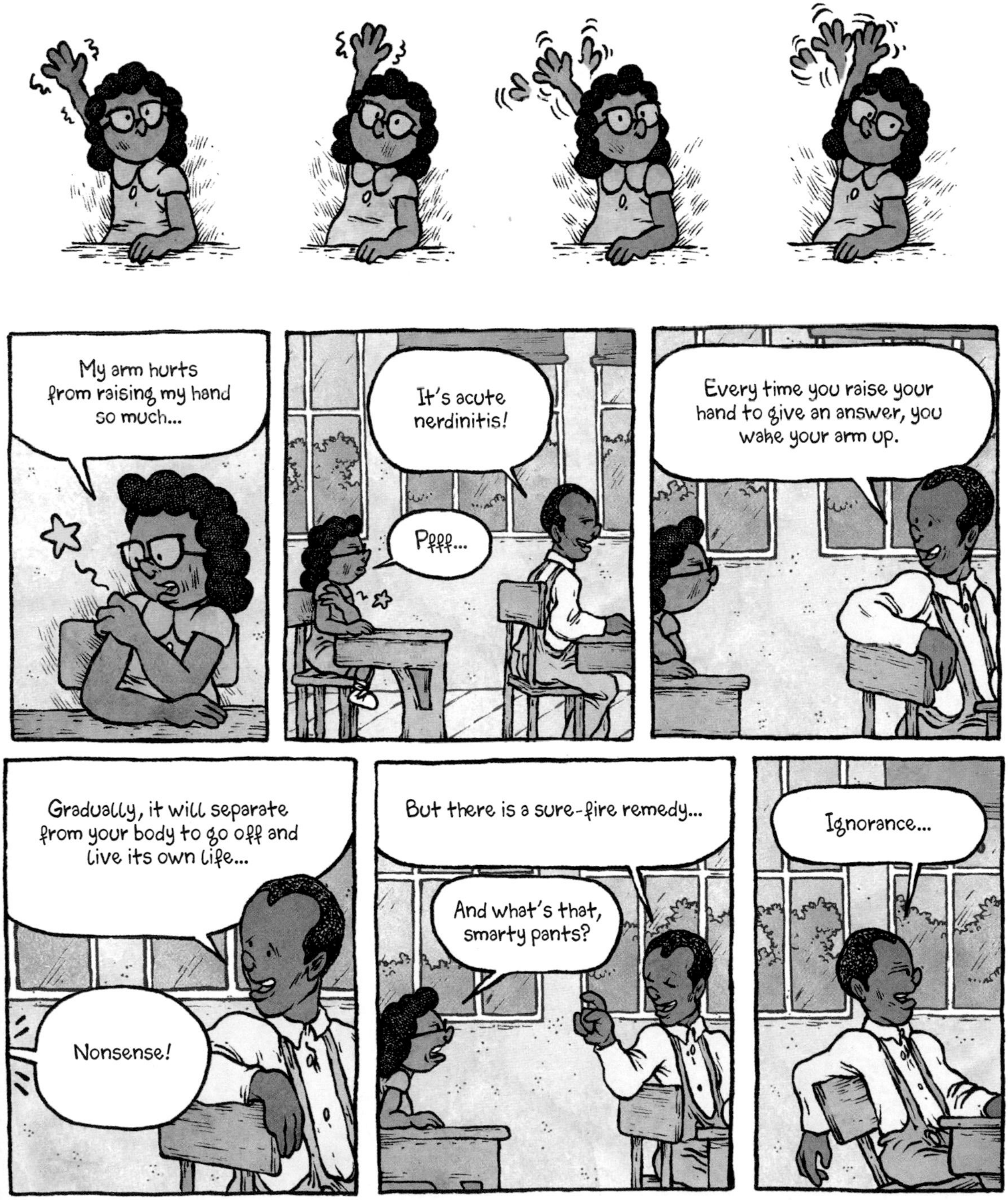

My arm hurts from raising my hand so much...
It's acute nerdinitis!
Pfff...
Every time you raise your hand to give an answer, you wake your arm up.
Gradually, it will separate from your body to go off and live its own life...
Nonsense!
But there is a sure-fire remedy...
And what's that, smarty pants?
Ignorance...

Zero To Zero

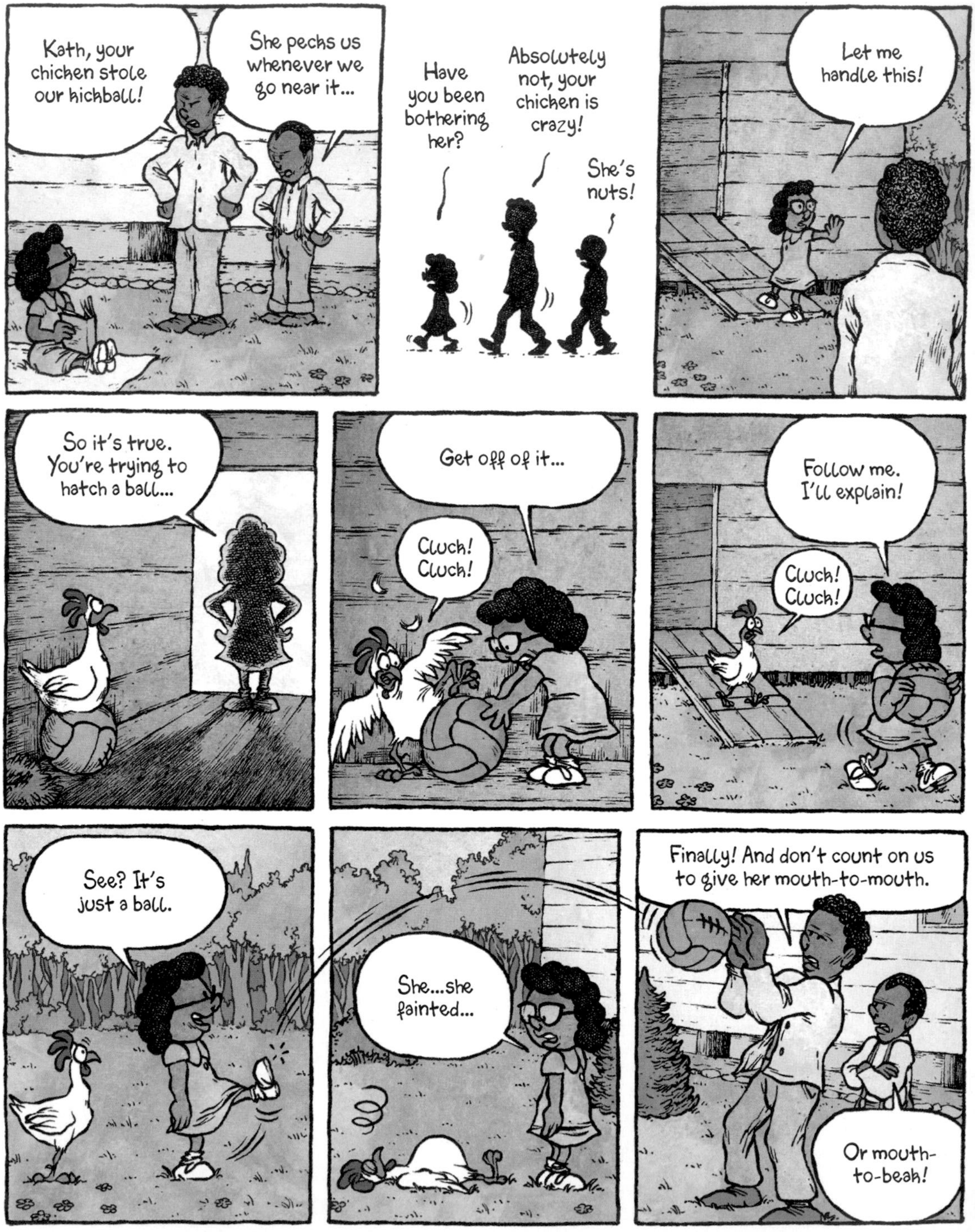

Kath, your chicken stole our kickball!
She pecks us whenever we go near it...
Have you been bothering her?
Absolutely not, your chicken is crazy!
She's nuts!
Let me handle this!
So it's true. You're trying to hatch a ball...
Get off of it...
Cluck! Cluck!
Follow me. I'll explain!
Cluck! Cluck!
See? It's just a ball.
She...she fainted...
Finally! And don't count on us to give her mouth-to-mouth.
Or mouth-to-beak!

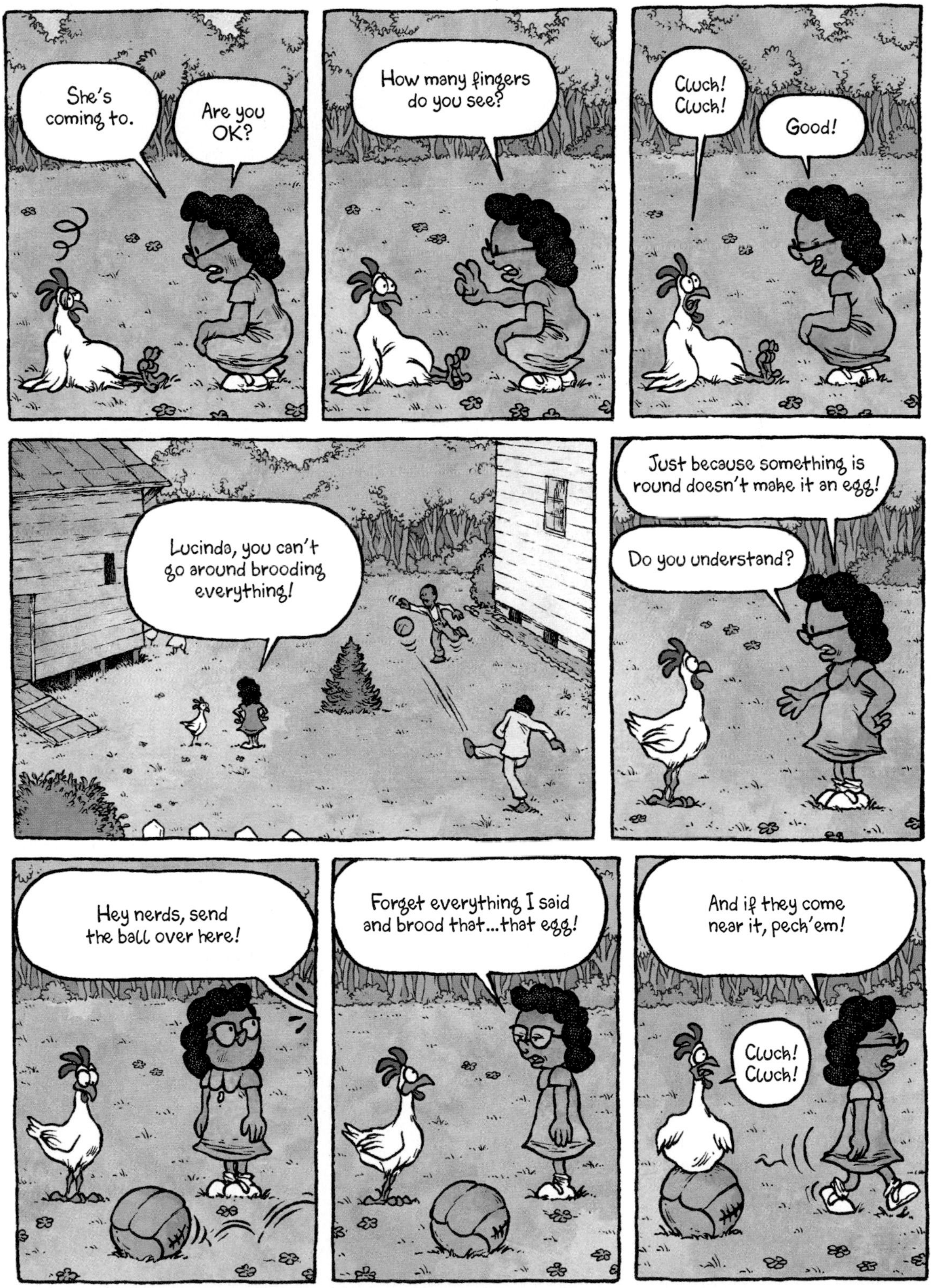
She's coming to.
Are you OK?
How many fingers do you see?
Cluck! Cluck!
Good!
Lucinda, you can't go around brooding everything!
Just because something is round doesn't make it an egg!
Do you understand?
Hey nerds, send the ball over here!
Forget everything I said and brood that...that egg!
And if they come near it, peck'em!
Cluck! Cluck!

6,786

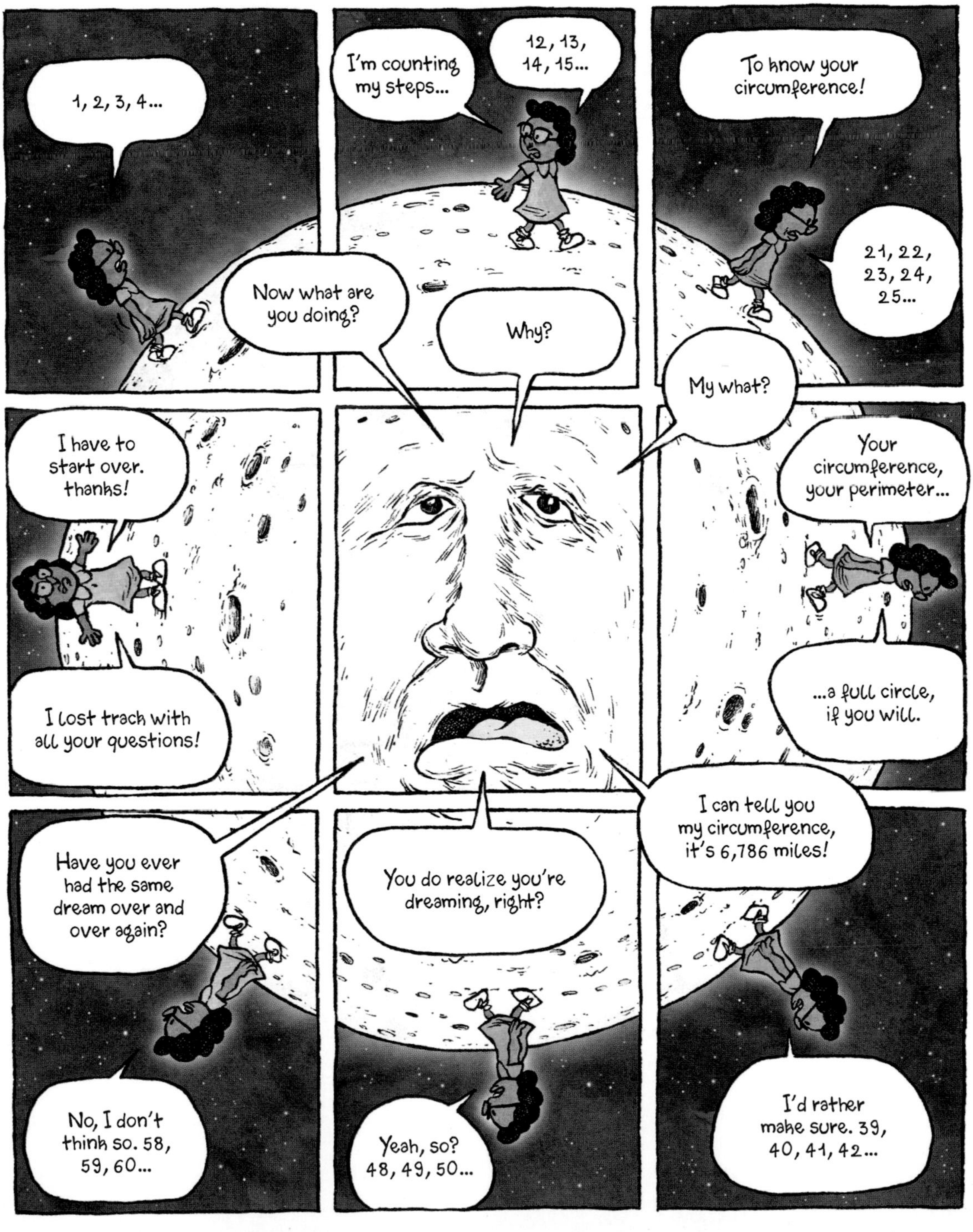

1, 2, 3, 4...
I'm counting my steps...
12, 13, 14, 15...
Now what are you doing?
Why?
To know your circumference!
21, 22, 23, 24, 25...
My what?
Your circumference, your perimeter...
...a full circle, if you will.
I can tell you my circumference, it's 6,786 miles!
I have to start over. thanks!
I lost track with all your questions!
You do realize you're dreaming, right?
Yeah, so? 48, 49, 50...
Have you ever had the same dream over and over again?
No, I don't think so. 58, 59, 60...
I'd rather make sure. 39, 40, 41, 42...

1 1/2 Hours

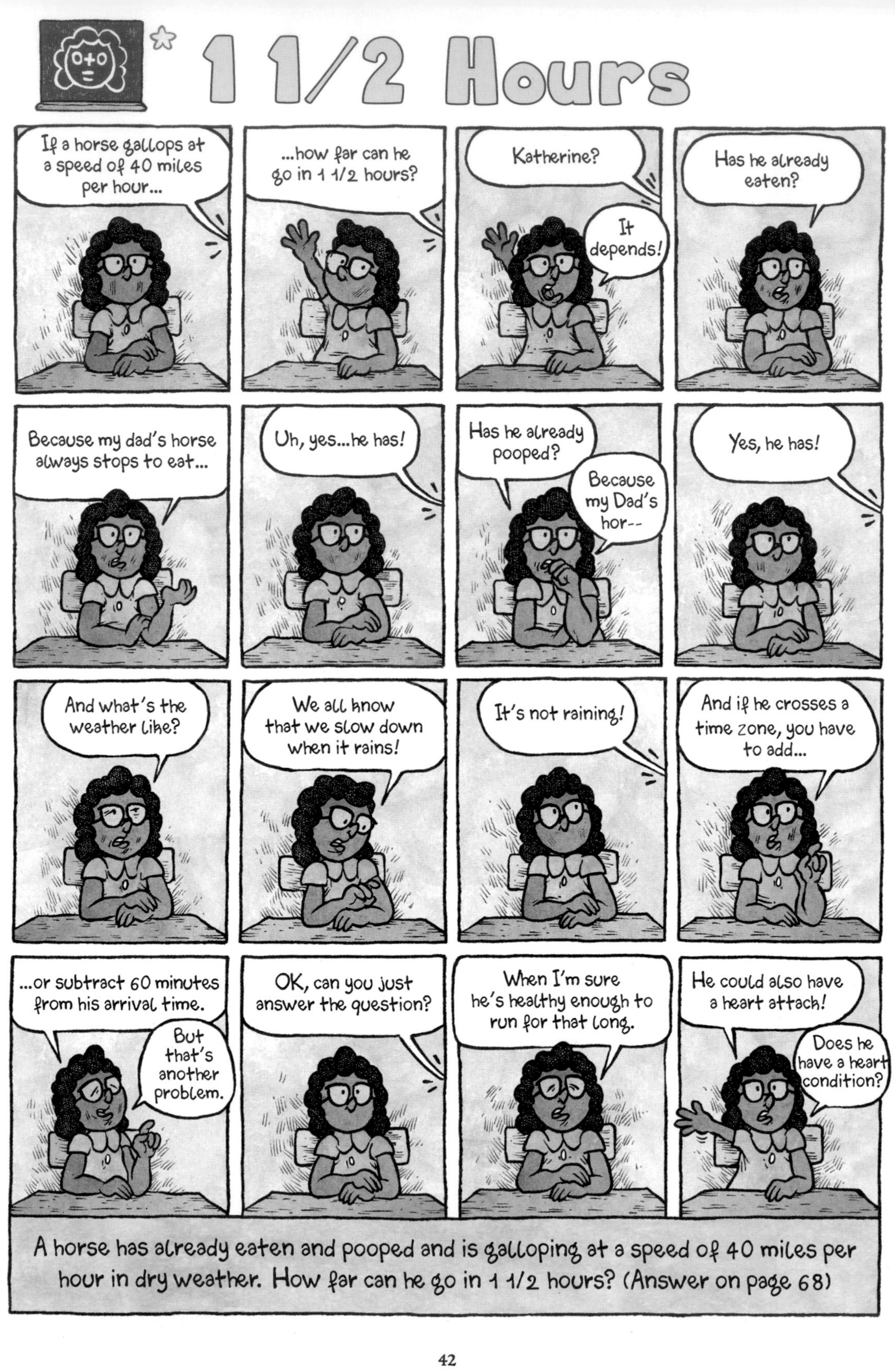
If a horse gallops at a speed of 40 miles per hour...
...how far can he go in 1 1/2 hours?
Katherine?
It depends!
Has he already eaten?
Because my dad's horse always stops to eat...
Uh, yes...he has!
Has he already pooped?
Because my Dad's hor--
Yes, he has!
And what's the weather like?
We all know that we slow down when it rains!
It's not raining!
And if he crosses a time zone, you have to add...
...or subtract 60 minutes from his arrival time.
But that's another problem.
OK, can you just answer the question?
When I'm sure he's healthy enough to run for that long.
He could also have a heart attack!
Does he have a heart condition?

A horse has already eaten and pooped and is galloping at a speed of 40 miles per hour in dry weather. How far can he go in 1 1/2 hours? (Answer on page 68)

7

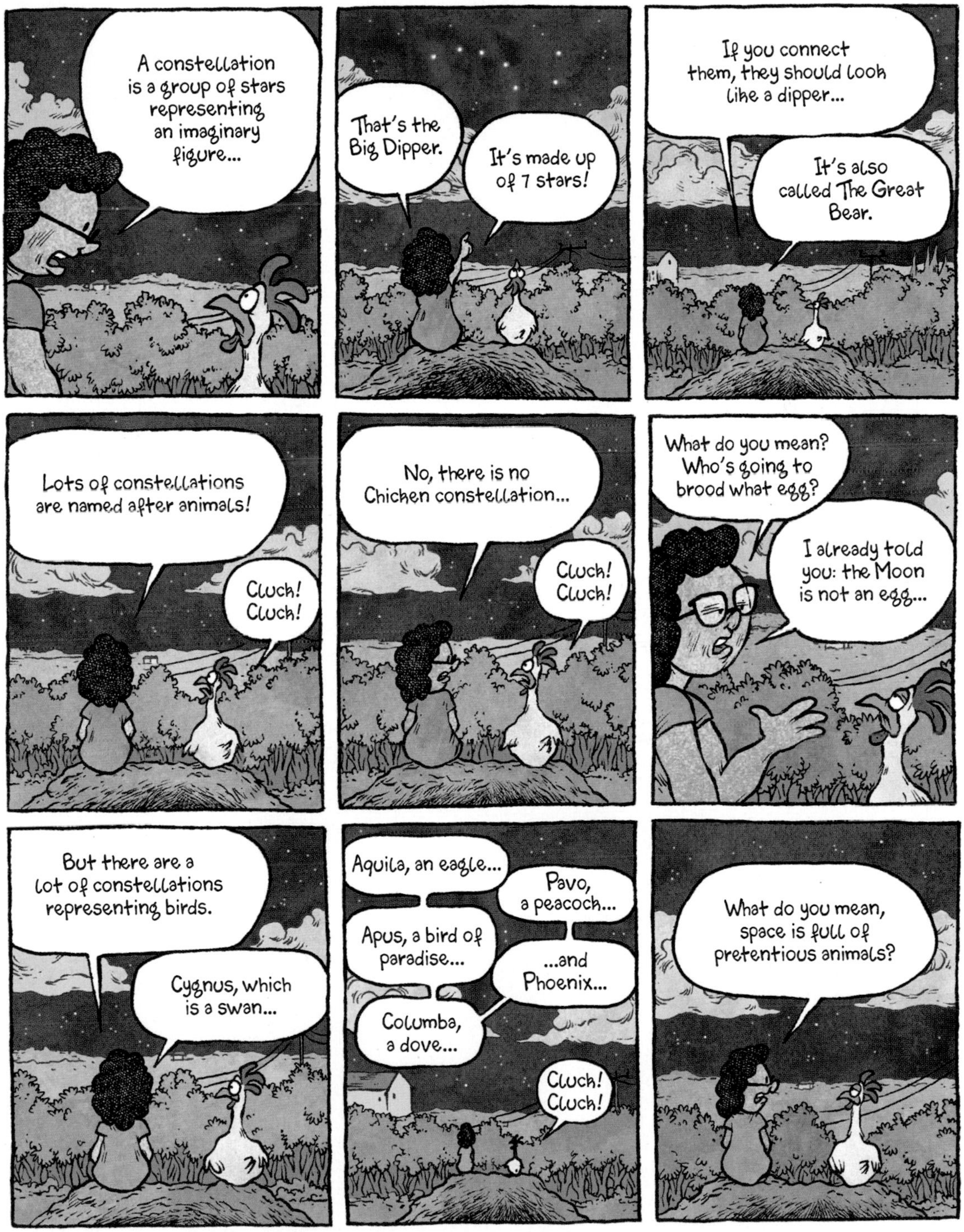
A constellation is a group of stars representing an imaginary figure...
That's the Big Dipper.
It's made up of 7 stars!
If you connect them, they should look like a dipper...
It's also called The Great Bear.
Lots of constellations are named after animals!
Cluck! Cluck!
No, there is no Chicken constellation...
Cluck! Cluck!
What do you mean? Who's going to brood what egg?
I already told you: the Moon is not an egg...
But there are a lot of constellations representing birds.
Cygnus, which is a swan...
Aquila, an eagle...
Pavo, a peacock...
Apus, a bird of paradise...
...and Phoenix...
Columba, a dove...
Cluck! Cluck!
What do you mean, space is full of pretentious animals?

Milk+Chocolate=

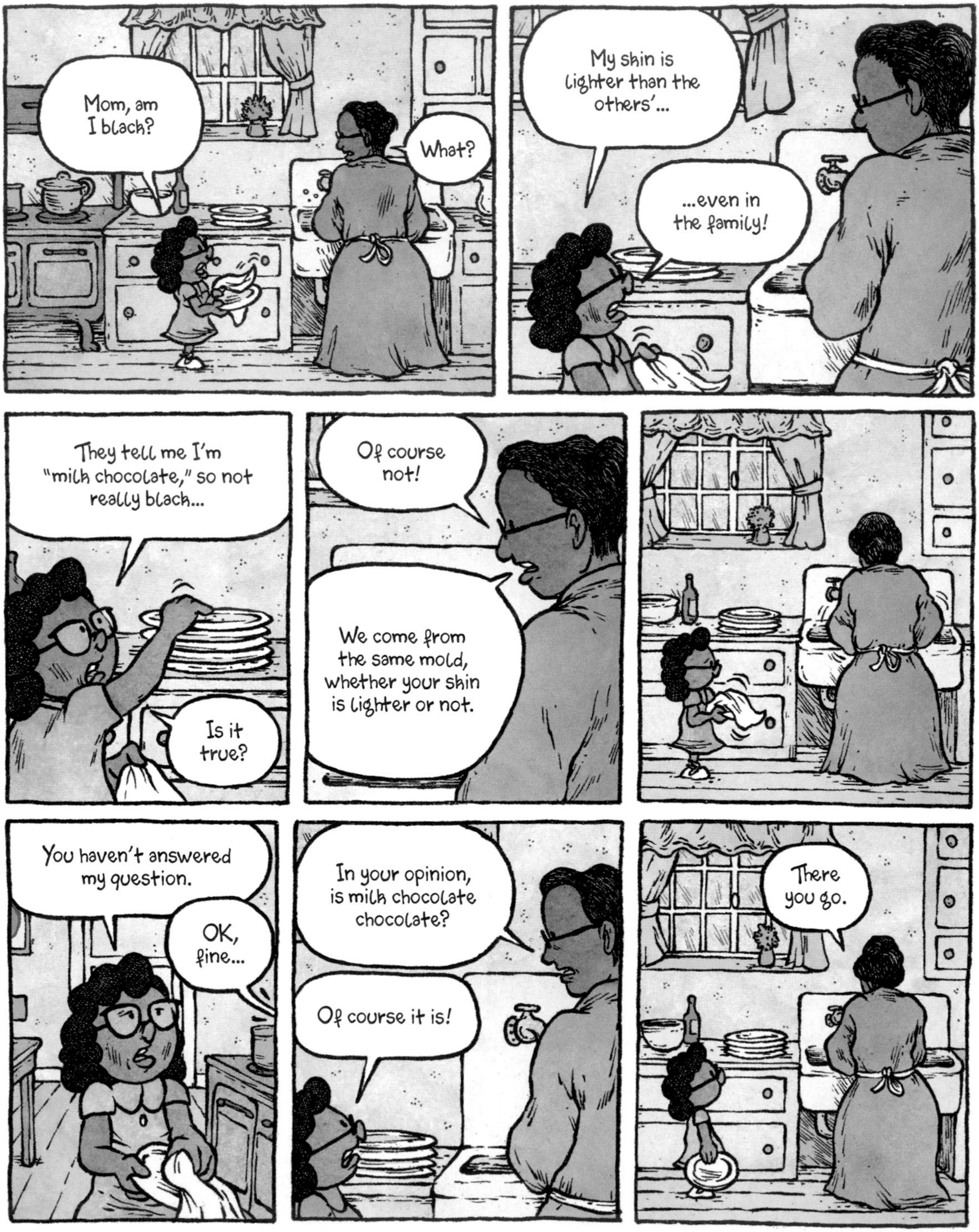
Mom, am I black?
What?
My skin is lighter than the others'...
...even in the family!
They tell me I'm "milk chocolate," so not really black...
Is it true?
Of course not!
We come from the same mold, whether your skin is lighter or not.
You haven't answered my question.
OK, fine...
In your opinion, is milk chocolate chocolate?
Of course it is!
There you go.

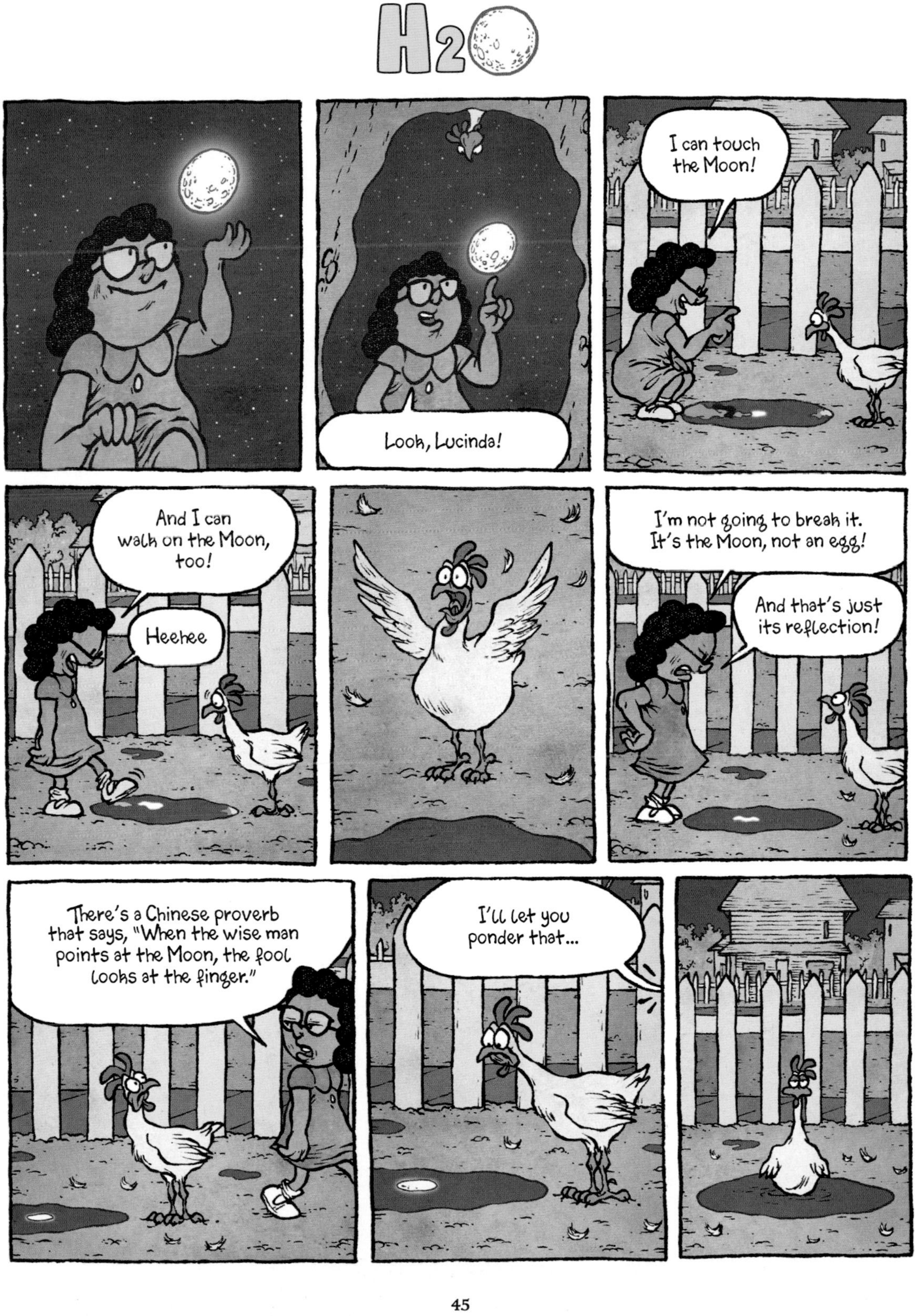
H2O
Look, Lucinda!
I can touch the Moon!
And I can walk on the Moon, too!
Heehee
I'm not going to break it. It's the Moon, not an egg!
And that's just its reflection!
There's a Chinese proverb that says, "When the wise man points at the Moon, the fool looks at the finger."
I'll let you ponder that...

1.5 Quarts

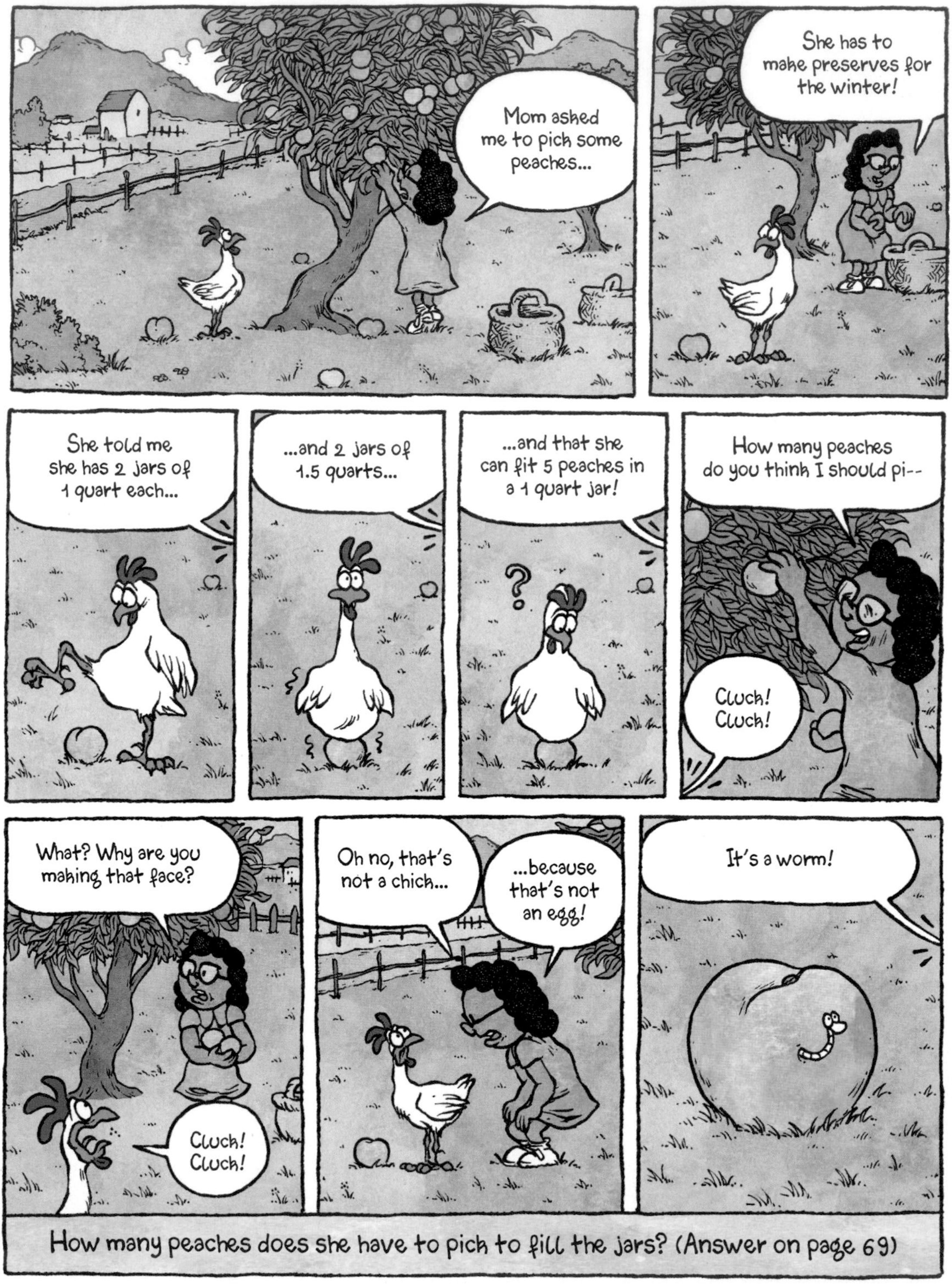

Mom asked me to pick some peaches...
She has to make preserves for the winter!
She told me she has 2 jars of 1 quart each...
...and 2 jars of 1.5 quarts...
...and that she can fit 5 peaches in a 1 quart jar!
How many peaches do you think I should pi--
Cluck! Cluck!
What? Why are you making that face?
Cluck! Cluck!
Oh no, that's not a chick...
...because that's not an egg!
It's a worm!
How many peaches does she have to pick to fill the jars? (Answer on page 69)

C=?

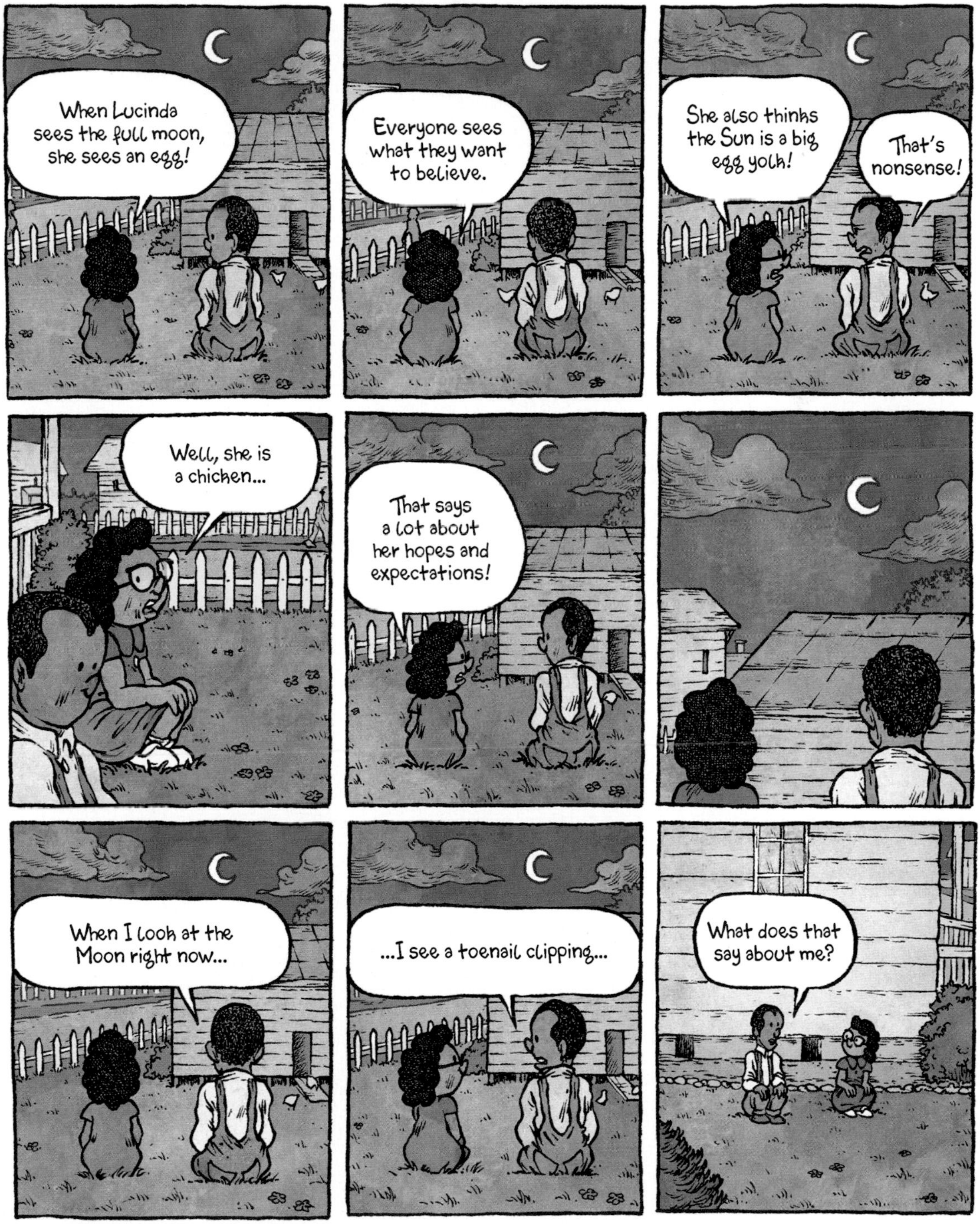
When Lucinda sees the full moon, she sees an egg!
Everyone sees what they want to believe.
She also thinks the Sun is a big egg yolk!
That's nonsense!
Well, she is a chicken...
That says a lot about her hopes and expectations!
When I look at the Moon right now...
...I see a toenail clipping...
What does that say about me?

18

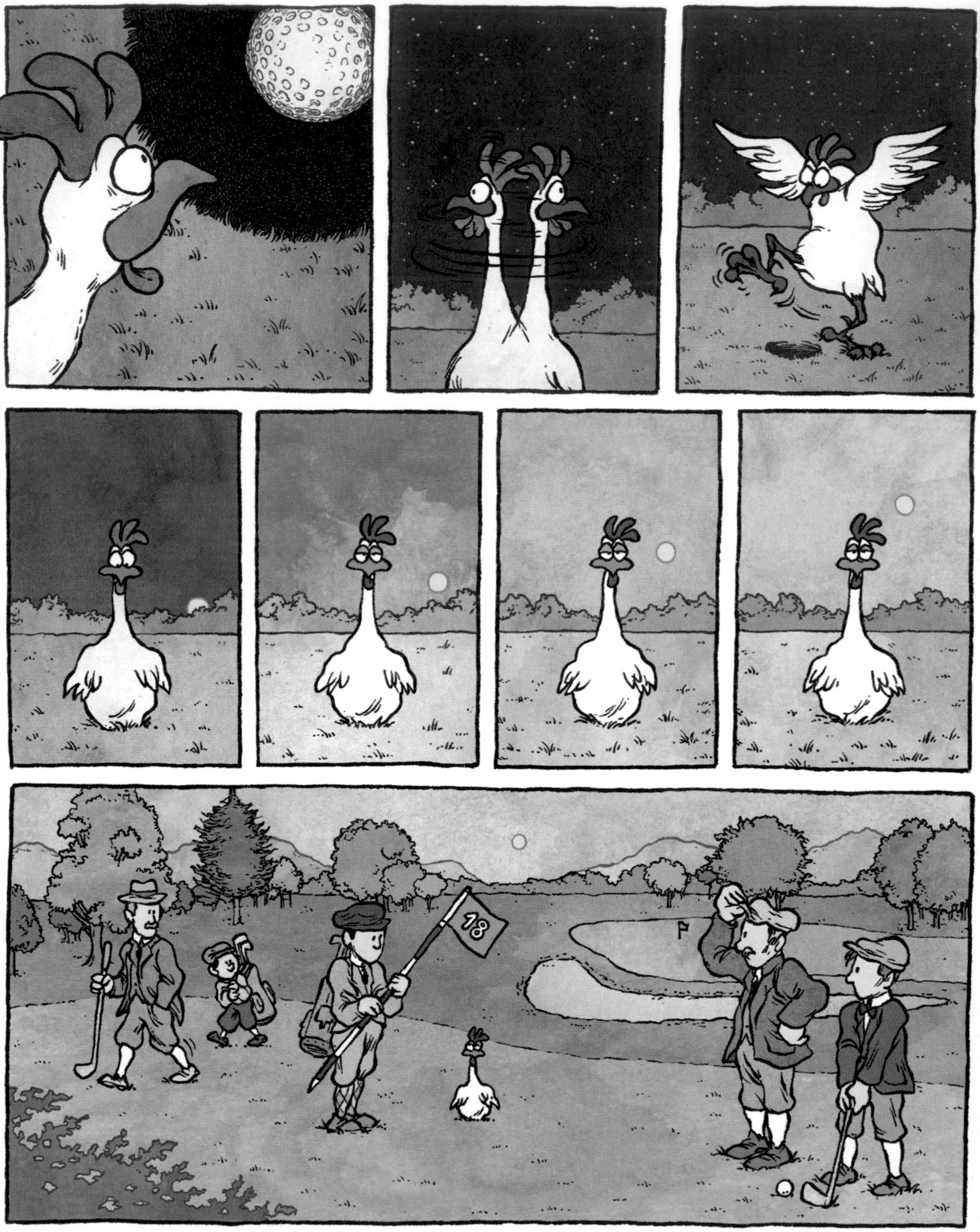
18

Hello, Katherine!

Hello, Mr. Olesen!

GLING!

What can I do for you today?

I'd like some candy.

Since I have 32 cents, I'll take 16 lollipops that cost 1 cent each...

...and 8 jujyfruits that cost 2 cents each...

That's 24 pieces of candy!

My sister, my two brothers, and I will be able to split them all evenly.

Here you go, I put everything in this bag for you. Enjoy!

Thanks, see you soon!

That little Coleman is so good with numbers, she's going to go places...

GLING!

Yes, she'll make a wonderful grocer!

Y STORE

That's not exactly what I had in mind...

Grmbl...

How much candy will each sibling get? (Answer on page 69)

5¢

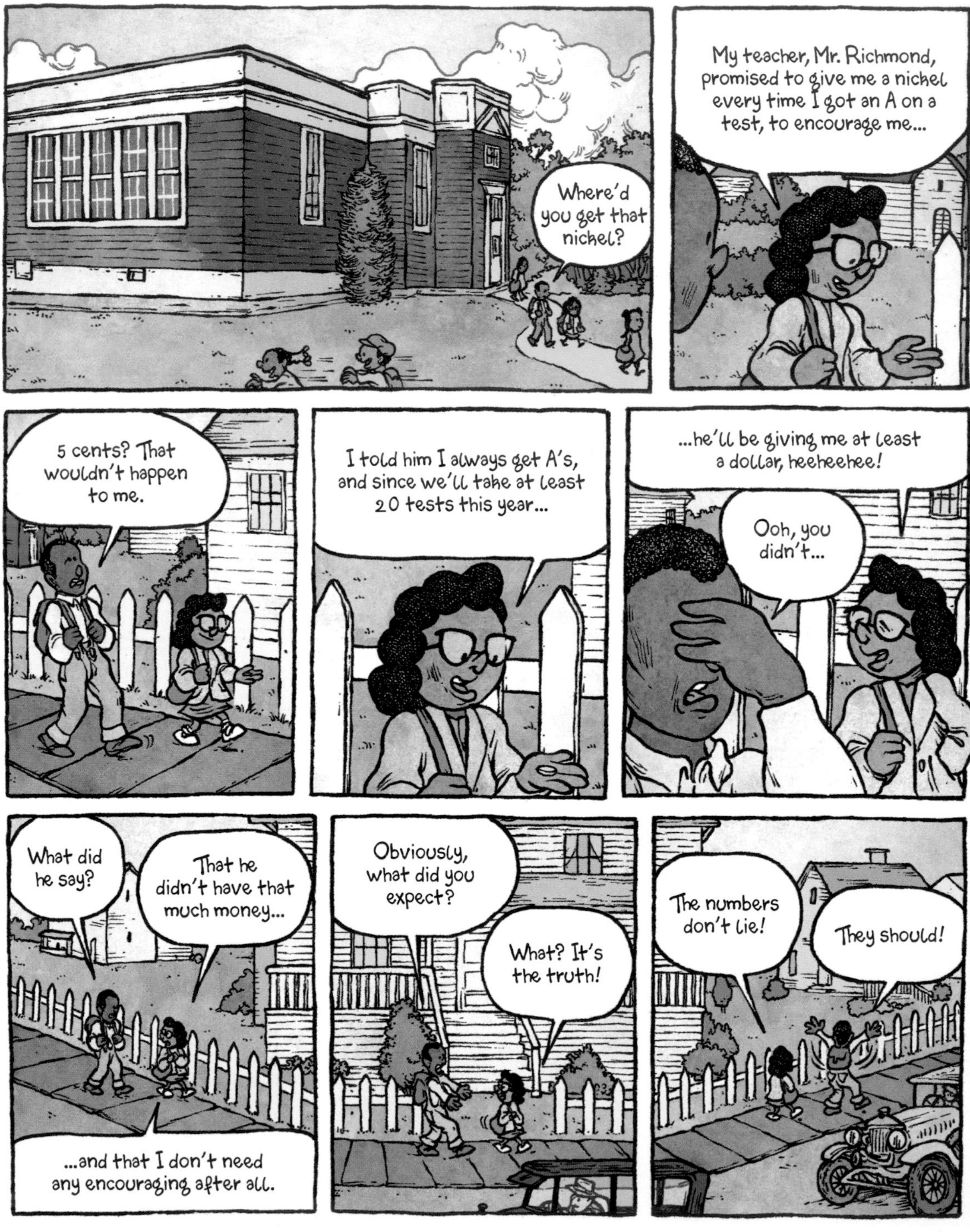
Where'd you get that nickel?
My teacher, Mr. Richmond, promised to give me a nickel every time I got an A on a test, to encourage me...
5 cents? That wouldn't happen to me.
I told him I always get A's, and since we'll take at least 20 tests this year...
...he'll be giving me at least a dollar, heeheehee!
Ooh, you didn't...
What did he say?
That he didn't have that much money...
...and that I don't need any encouraging after all.
Obviously, what did you expect?
What? It's the truth!
The numbers don't lie!
They should!

2 Inches

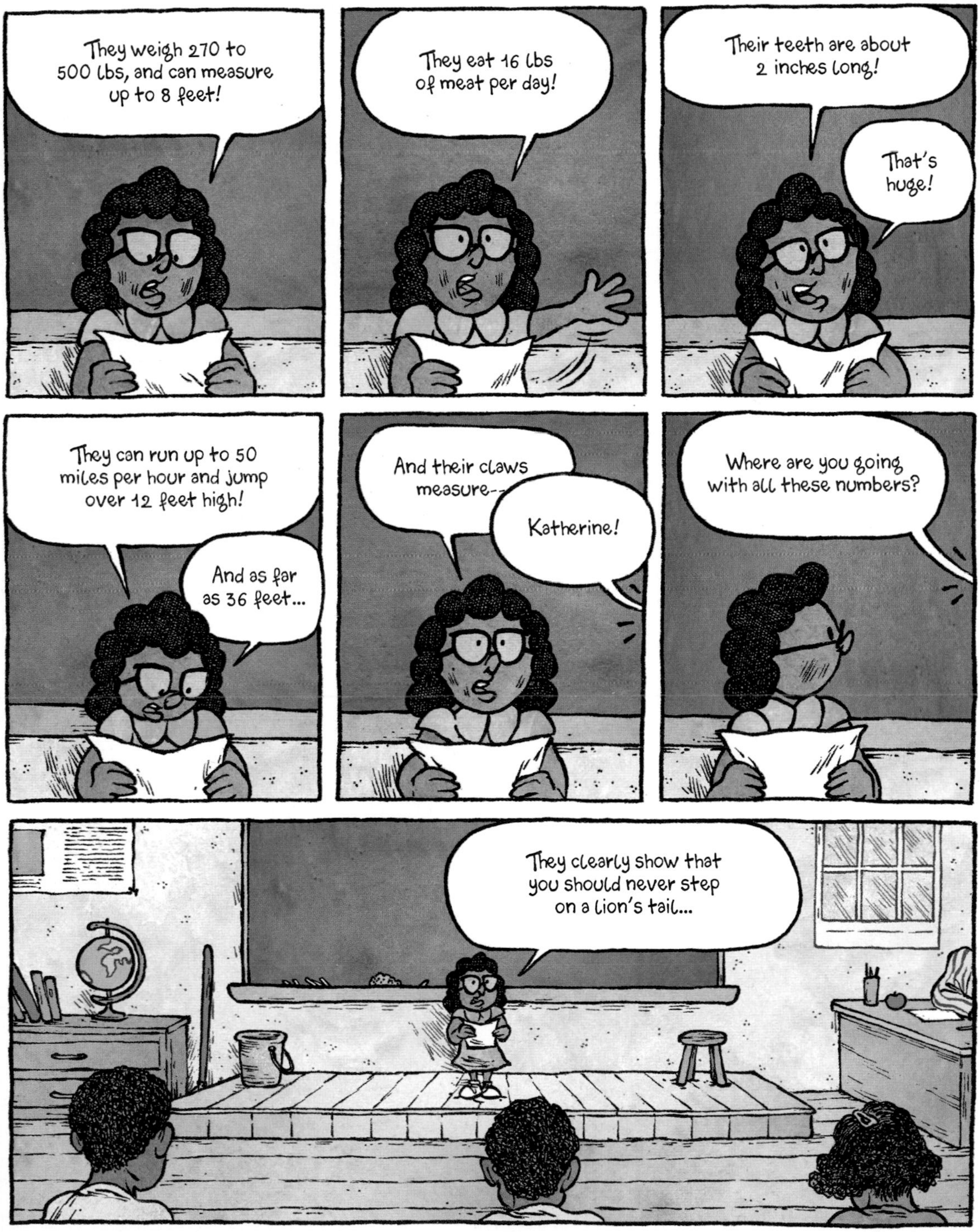
They weigh 270 to 500 lbs, and can measure up to 8 feet!
They eat 16 lbs of meat per day!
Their teeth are about 2 inches long!
That's huge!
They can run up to 50 miles per hour and jump over 12 feet high!
And as far as 36 feet...
And their claws measure--
Katherine!
Where are you going with all these numbers?
They clearly show that you should never step on a lion's tail...

6x

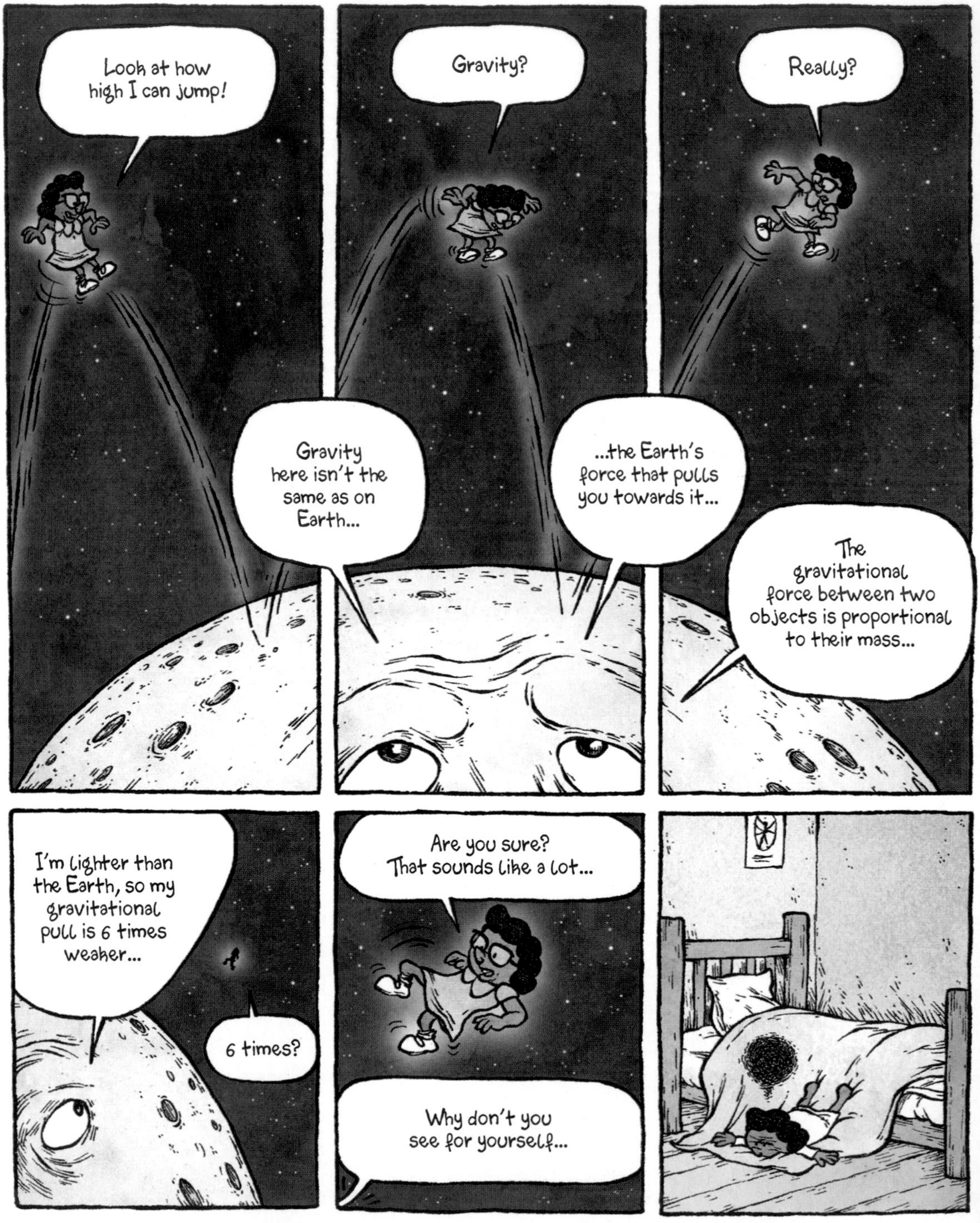
Look at how high I can jump!
Gravity?
Really?
Gravity here isn't the same as on Earth...
...the Earth's force that pulls you towards it...
The gravitational force between two objects is proportional to their mass...
I'm lighter than the Earth, so my gravitational pull is 6 times weaker...
6 times?
Are you sure? That sounds like a lot...
Why don't you see for yourself...

What's that?

Here, its for you!

Math... Of course...

Geometry!

And why did you draw all these triangles?

They're equilateral triangles!

Equilateral, what does that mean?

An equilateral triangle is a triangle with all 3 sides of equal length!

That still doesn't tell me why you drew these equi...equi...

Equilateral triangles! How many are there?

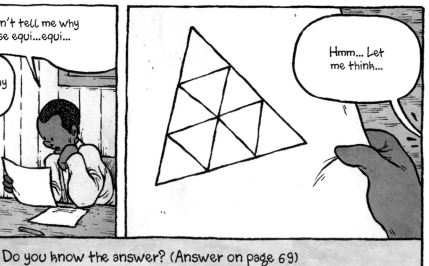

Hmm... Let me think...

Do you know the answer? (Answer on page 69)

24 Hours

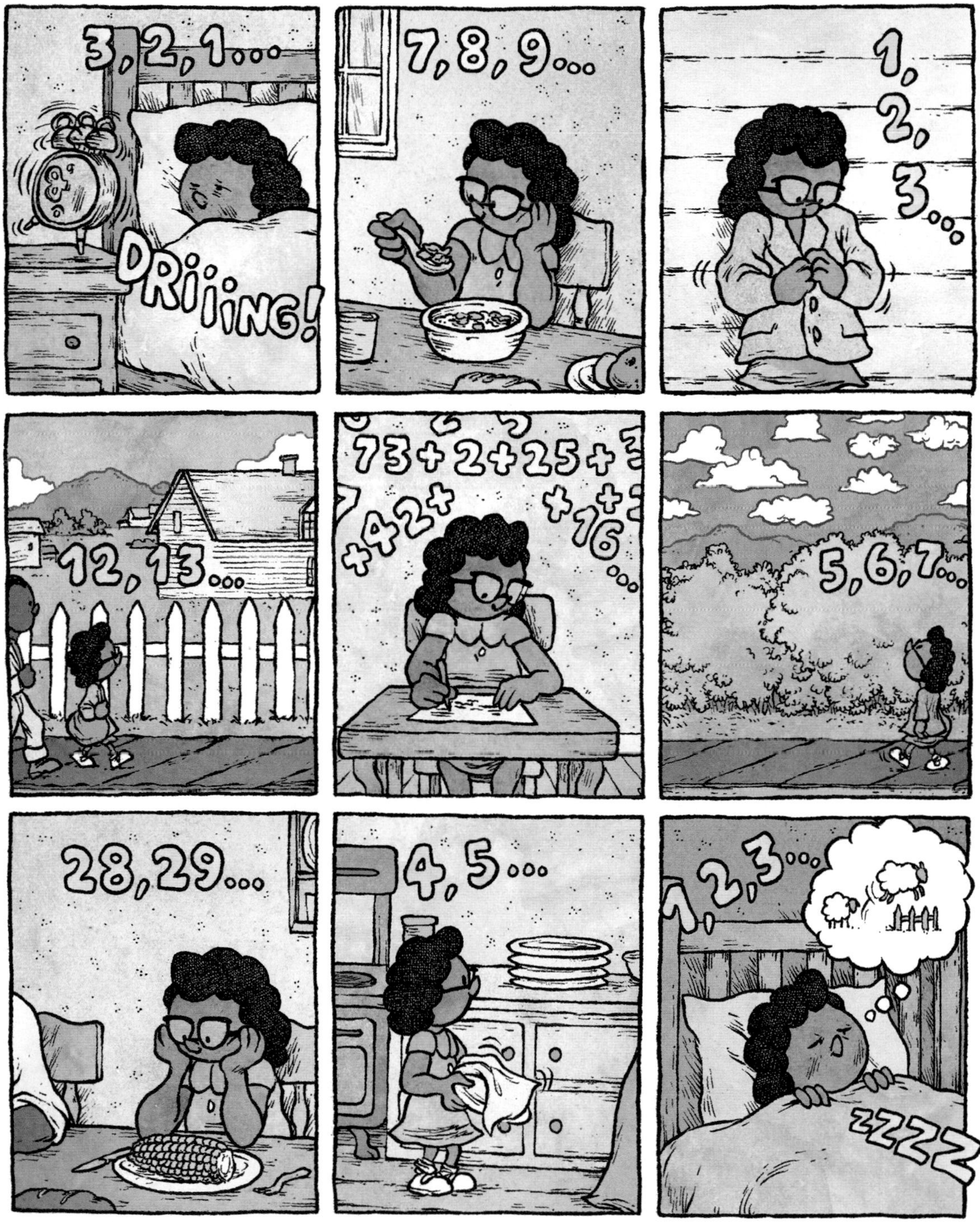

3, 2, 1...
DRiiiNG!
7, 8, 9...
1, 2, 3...
12, 13...
73+2+25+
+42+
+16...
5, 6, 7...
28, 29...
4, 5...
1, 2, 3...
ZZZZ

1, 2, 3... 3, 2, 1

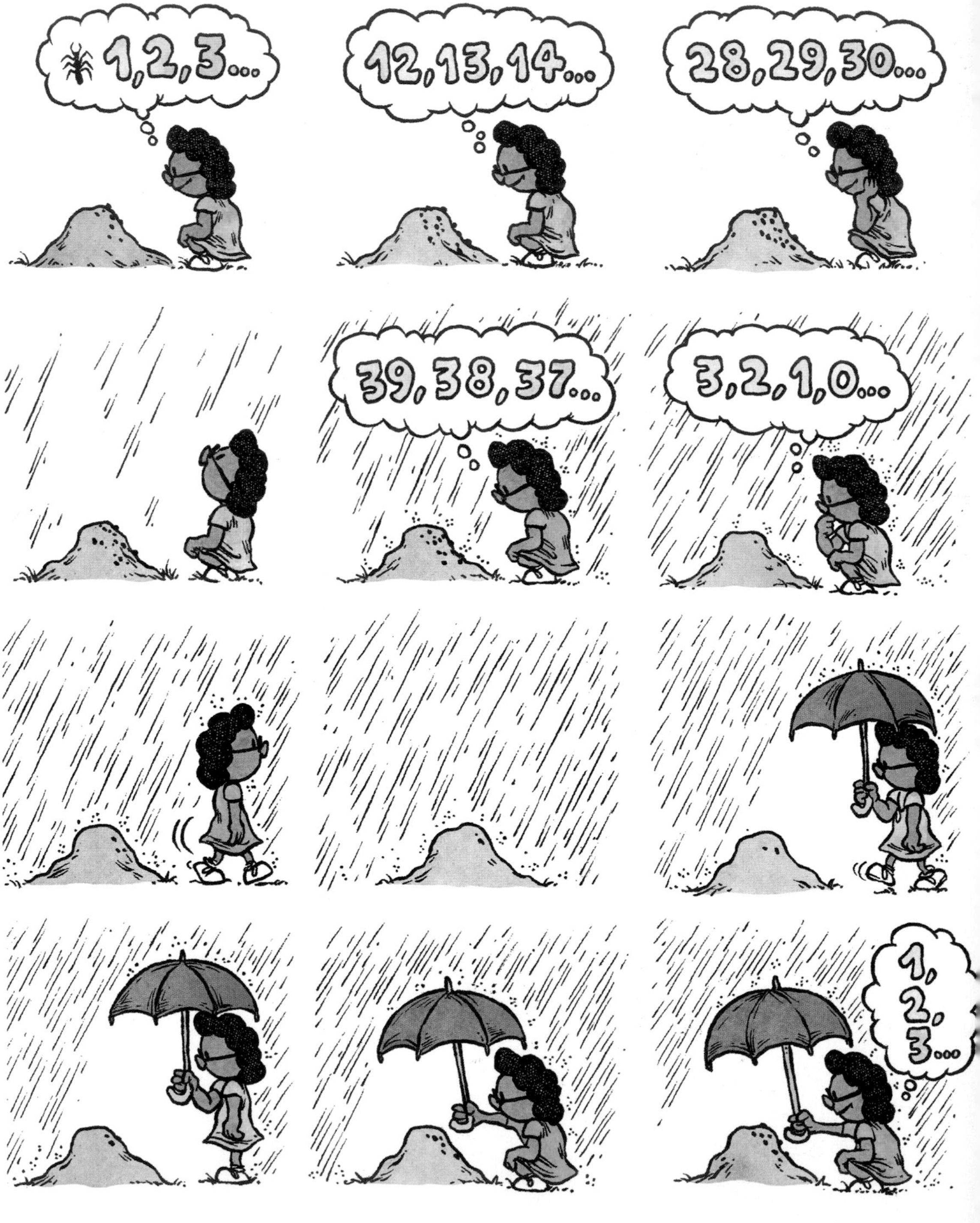

1,2,3...
12,13,14...
28,29,30...
39,38,37...
3,2,1,0...
1, 2, 3...

So did the chickens lay a lot of eggs this morning?

Not really...

There are 18 chickens. A third of them lay 1 egg per day.

Another third lay 1 egg every other day, half of them one day, the other half the next..

And none of the others have laid any eggs yet...

...except for Lucinda, who decided to lay an egg today!

Don't give the chickens names, we may have to eat them one day...

Not Lucinda!

Anyway, that doesn't tell me how many eggs you brought back.

Of course it does!

How many eggs has Katherine brought back this morning? (Answer on page 70)

11001011001

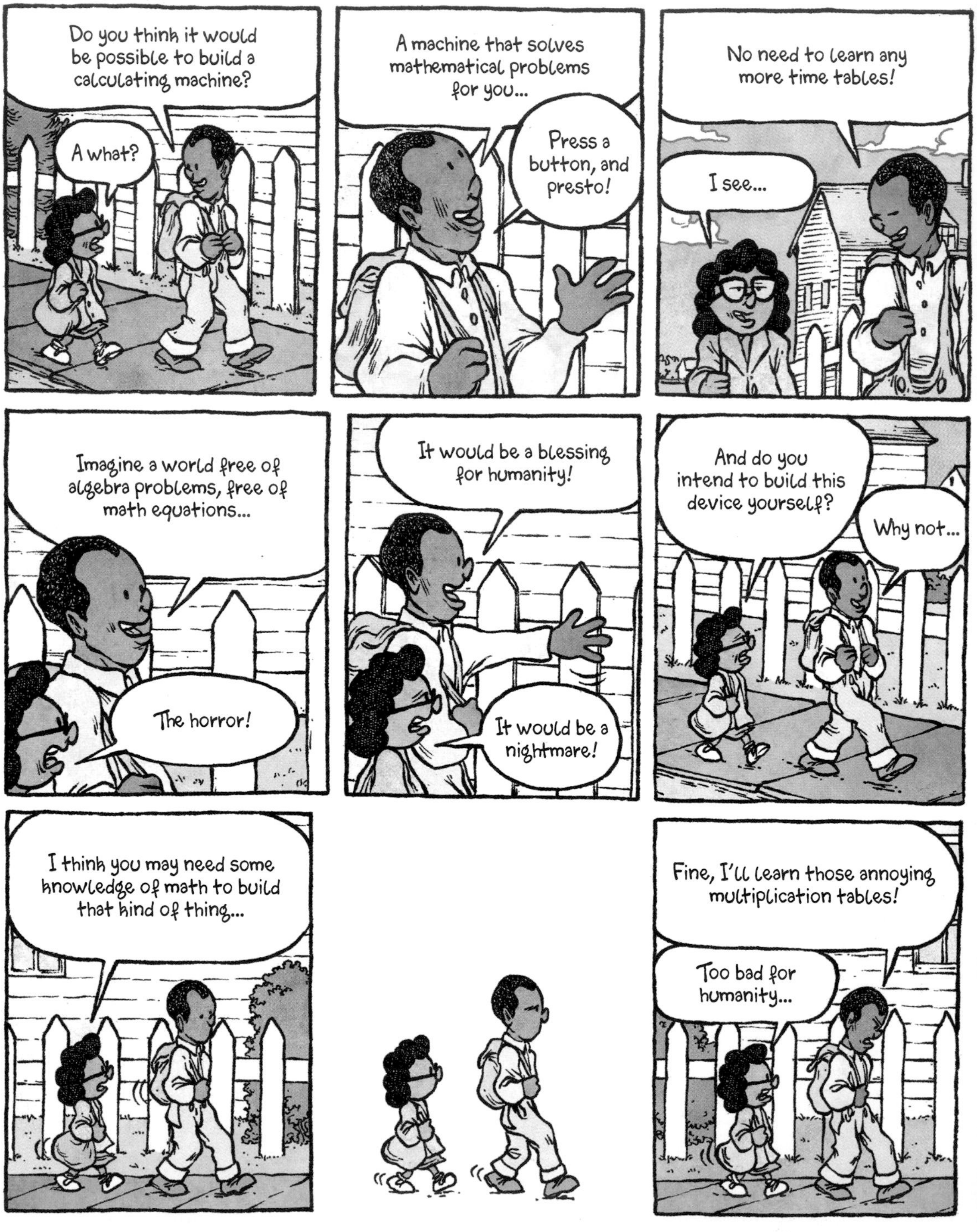
Do you think it would be possible to build a calculating machine?
A what?
A machine that solves mathematical problems for you...
Press a button, and presto!
No need to learn any more time tables!
I see...
Imagine a world free of algebra problems, free of math equations...
The horror!
It would be a blessing for humanity!
It would be a nightmare!
And do you intend to build this device yourself?
Why not...
I think you may need some knowledge of math to build that kind of thing...
Fine, I'll learn those annoying multiplication tables!
Too bad for humanity...

1971

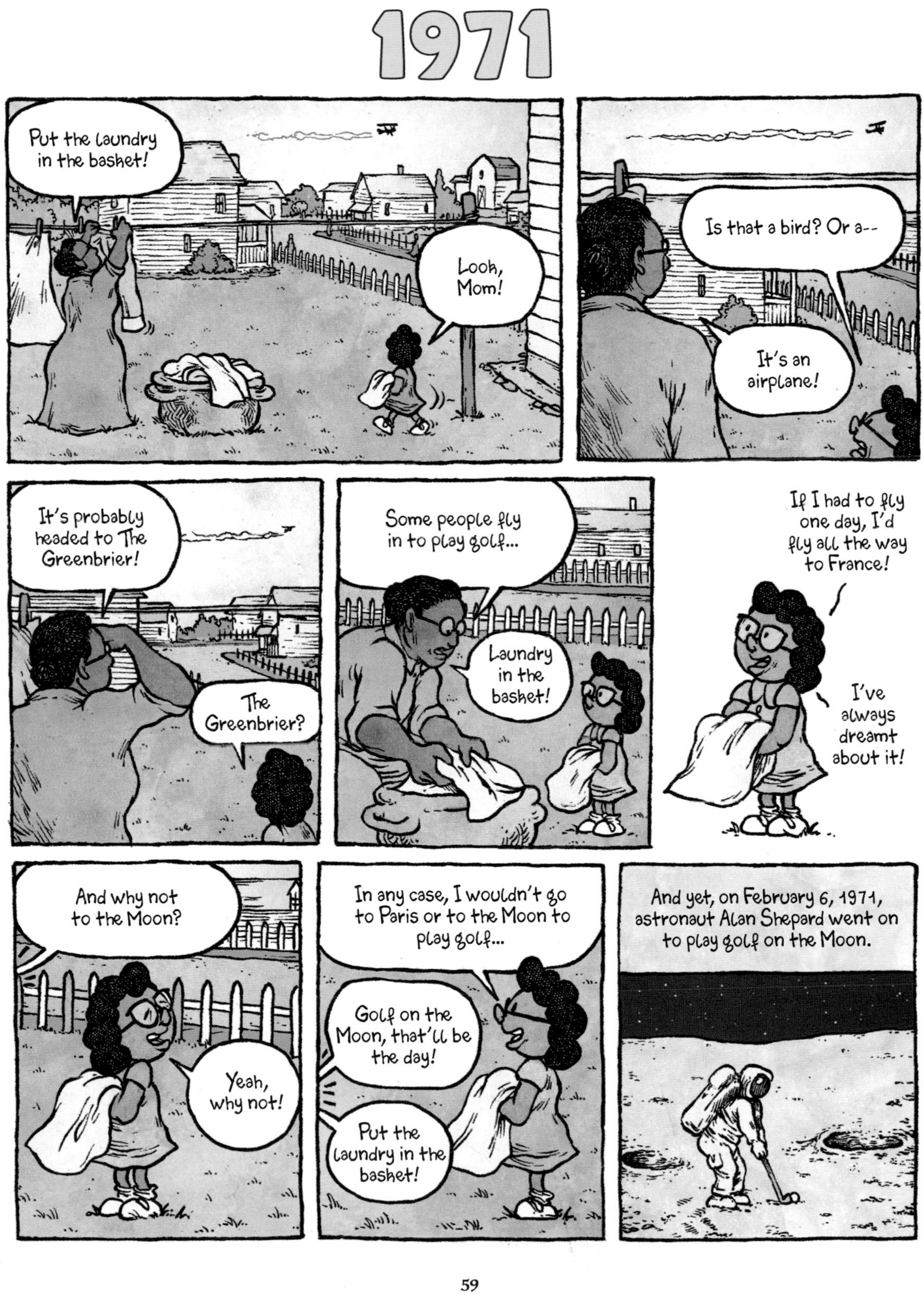

Put the laundry in the basket!
Look, Mom!
Is that a bird? Or a--
It's an airplane!
It's probably headed to The Greenbrier!
The Greenbrier?
Some people fly in to play golf...
Laundry in the basket!
If I had to fly one day, I'd fly all the way to France!
I've always dreamt about it!
And why not to the Moon?
Yeah, why not!
In any case, I wouldn't go to Paris or to the Moon to play golf...
Golf on the Moon, that'll be the day!
Put the laundry in the basket!
And yet, on February 6, 1971, astronaut Alan Shepard went on to play golf on the Moon.

It's mine!

No, I found it first!

What's going on?

I found a four-leaf clover and it's going to bring me good luck!

Nuh-uh, it's gonna bring ME good luck!

Now now, it's not the only one! There's one four-leaf clover for every 10,000 three-leaf clovers.

There are about 10,000 clovers per 10 square feet...

And since there are 100 square feet of clovers here, in the garden...

...that means--

WE DON'T CARE!

I want this one!

So do I, and it's mine!

Gimme back my good luck charm!

It's mine!

Having brothers is bad luck...

How many four-leaf clovers are there in the garden? (Answer on page 70)

1+1=2

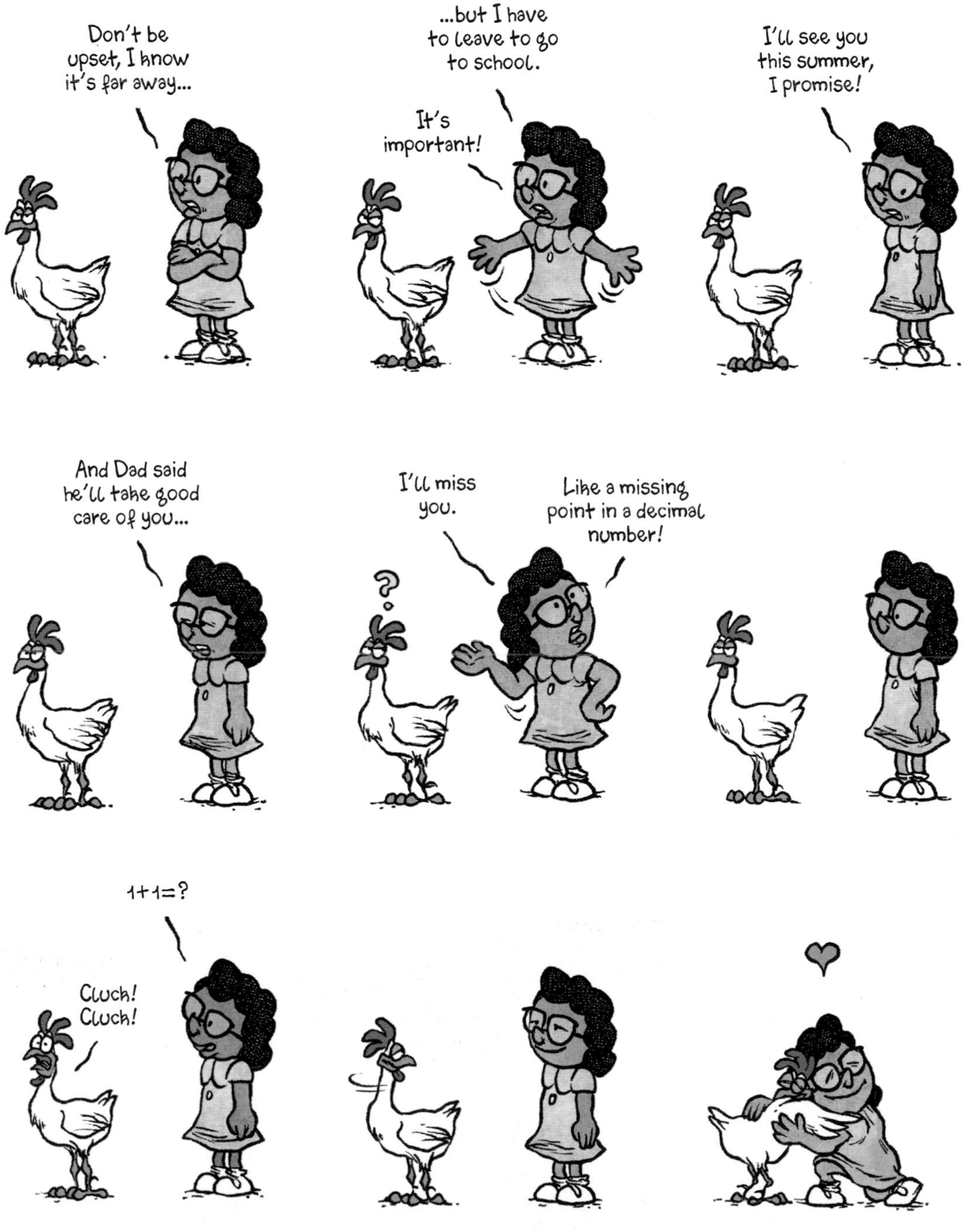

Don't be upset, I know it's far away...
...but I have to leave to go to school.
It's important!
I'll see you this summer, I promise!
And Dad said he'll take good care of you...
I'll miss you.
Like a missing point in a decimal number!
1+1=?
Cluck! Cluck!

x9

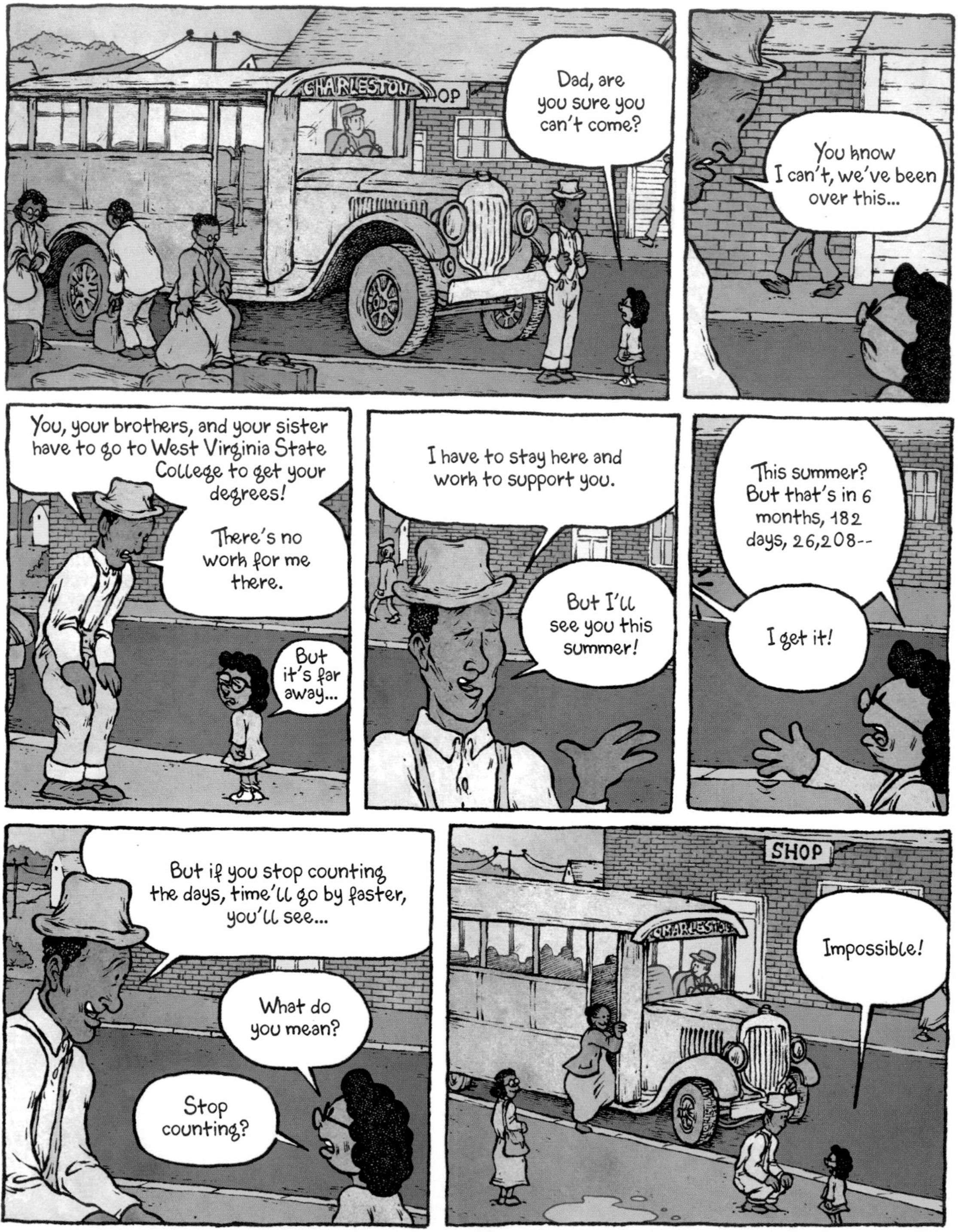
CHARLESTON
Dad, are you sure you can't come?
You know I can't, we've been over this...
You, your brothers, and your sister have to go to West Virginia State College to get your degrees!
There's no work for me there.
But it's far away...
I have to stay here and work to support you.
But I'll see you this summer!
This summer? But that's in 6 months, 182 days, 26,208--
I get it!
But if you stop counting the days, time'll go by faster, you'll see...
What do you mean?
Stop counting?
SHOP
CHARLESTON
Impossible!

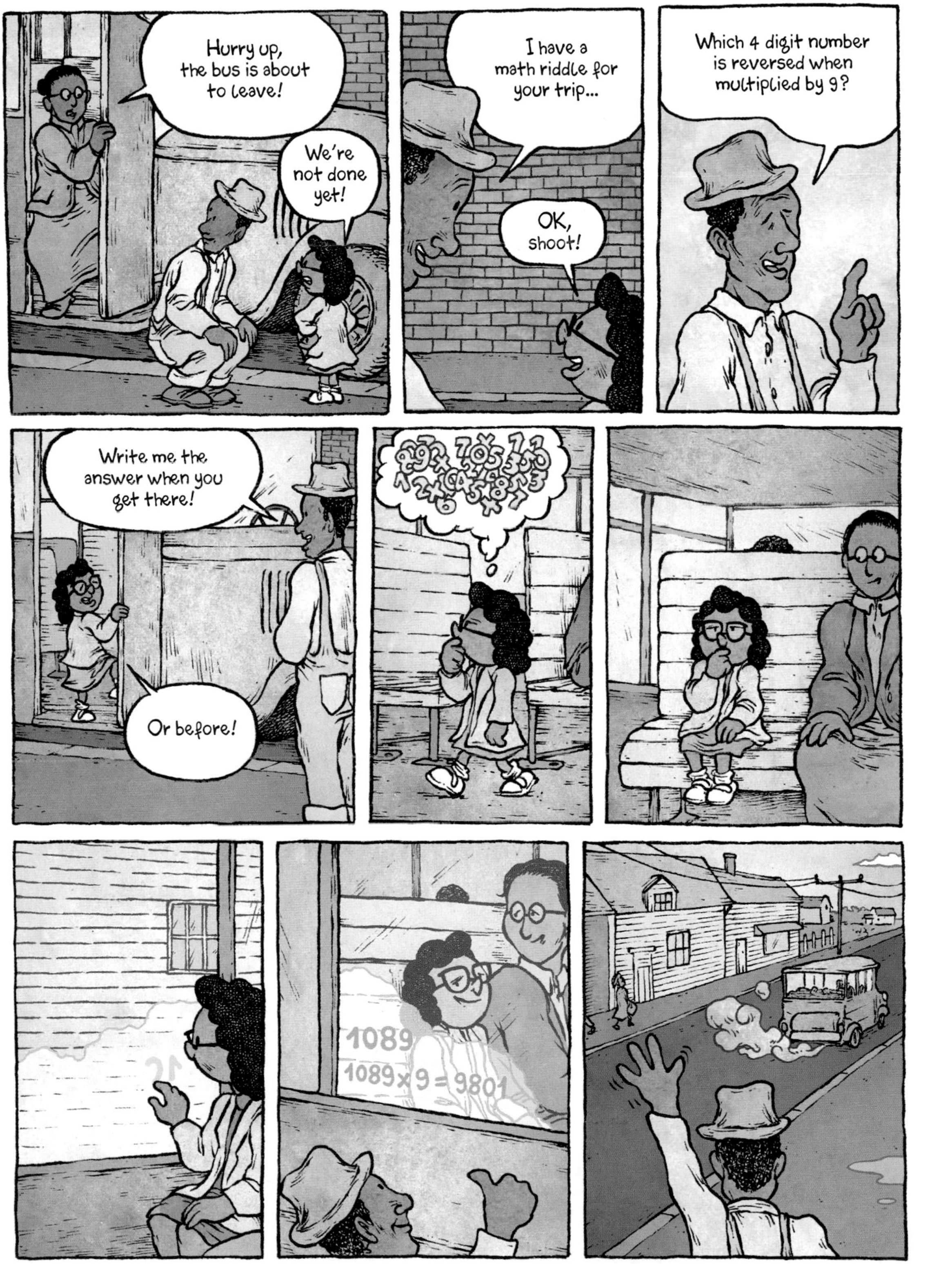
Hurry up, the bus is about to leave!
We're not done yet!
I have a math riddle for your trip...
OK, shoot!
Which 4 digit number is reversed when multiplied by 9?
Write me the answer when you get there!
Or before!
1089
1089 x 9 = 9801

Katherine Johnson graduated from high school at the age of 14.

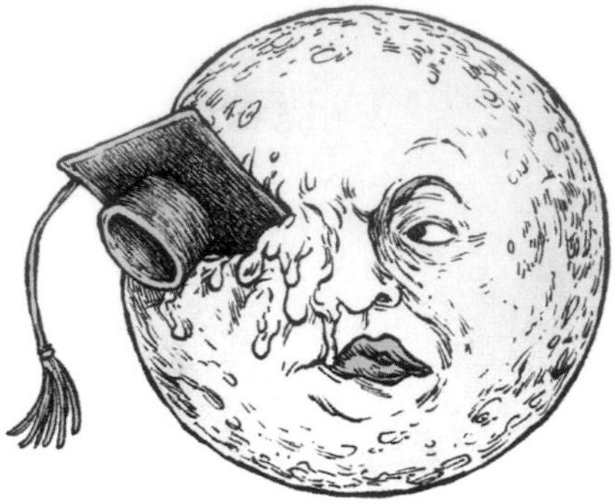

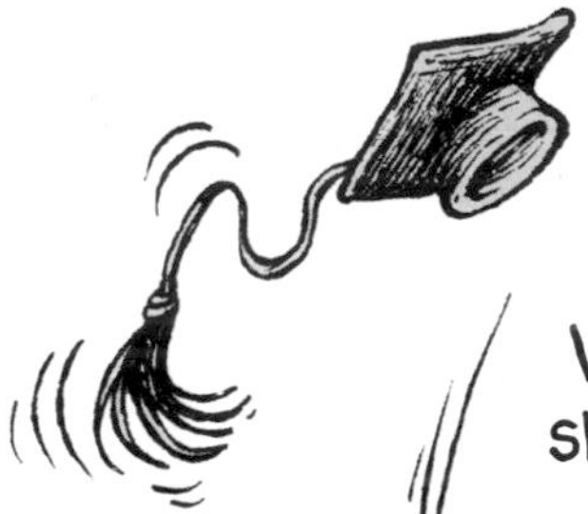

When she was 18, she graduated with highest honors from college with degrees in mathematics and French.

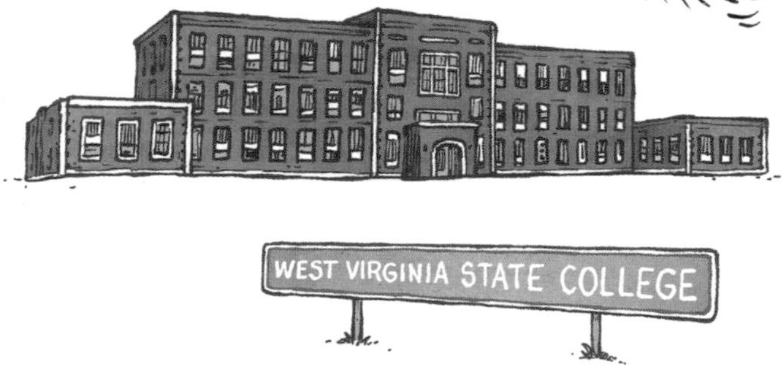
WEST VIRGINIA STATE COLLEGE

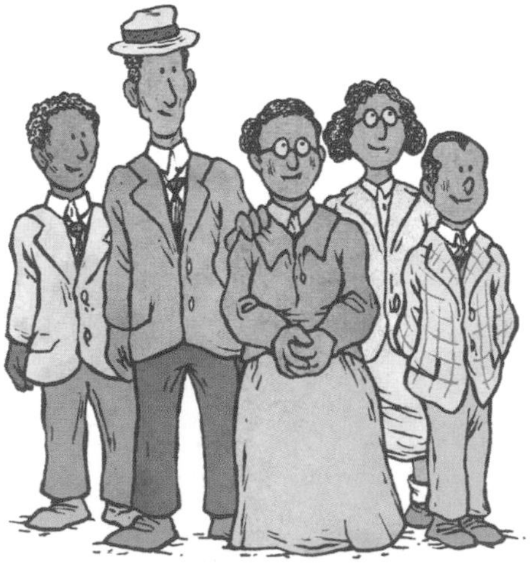

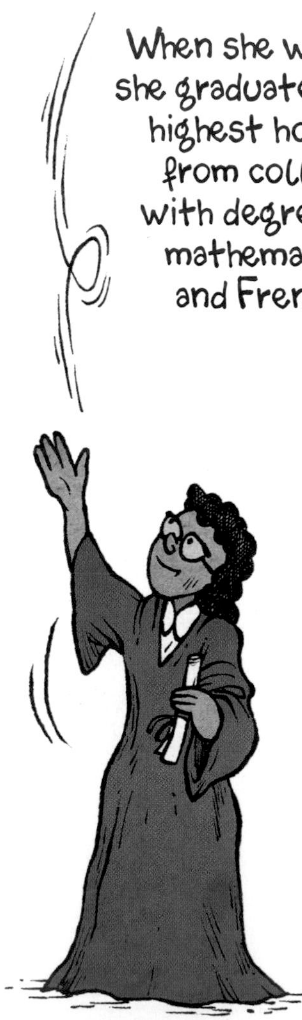

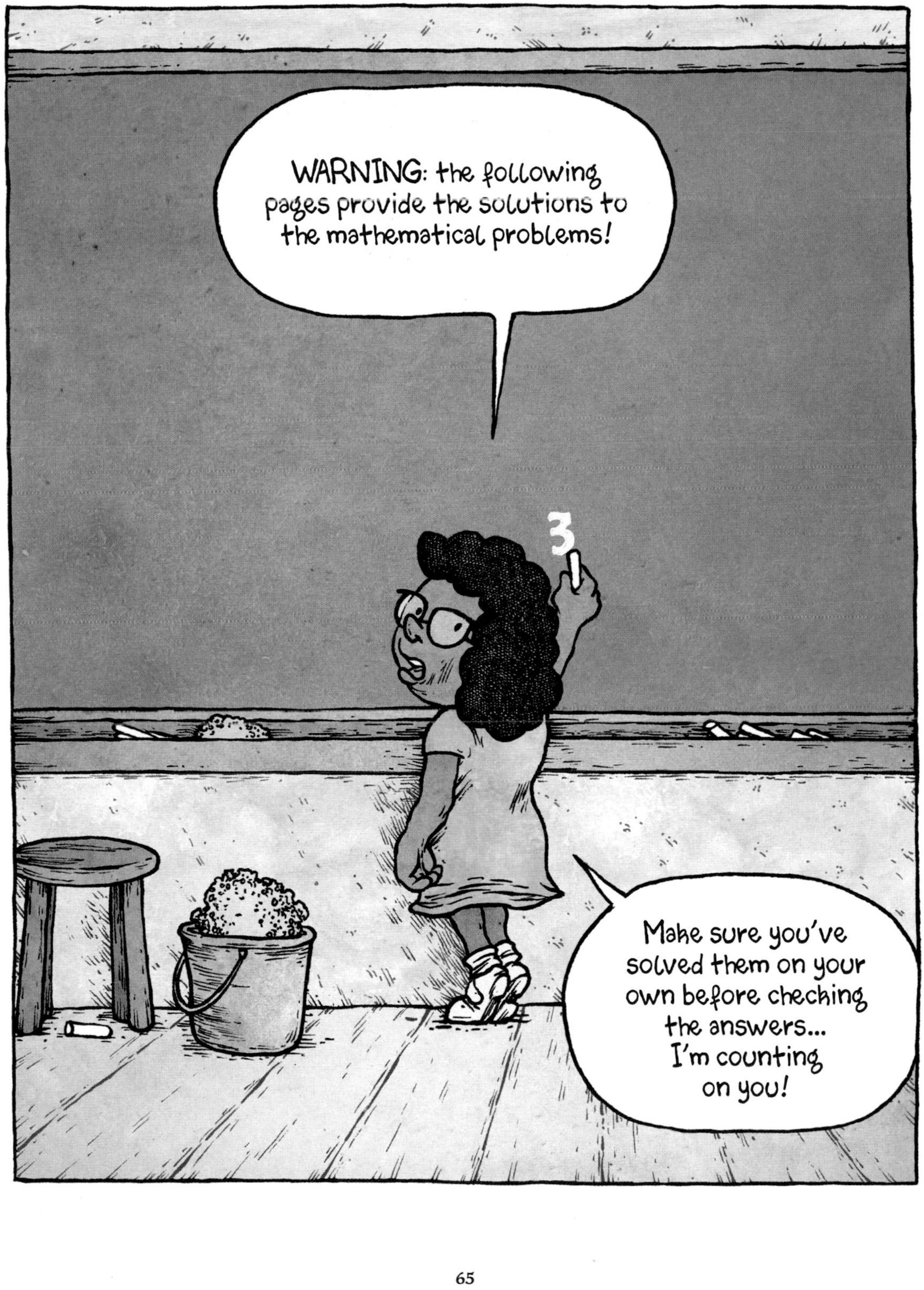

WARNING: the following pages provide the solutions to the mathematical problems!
3
Make sure you've solved them on your own before checking the answers... I'm counting on you!

Solution : 102°F

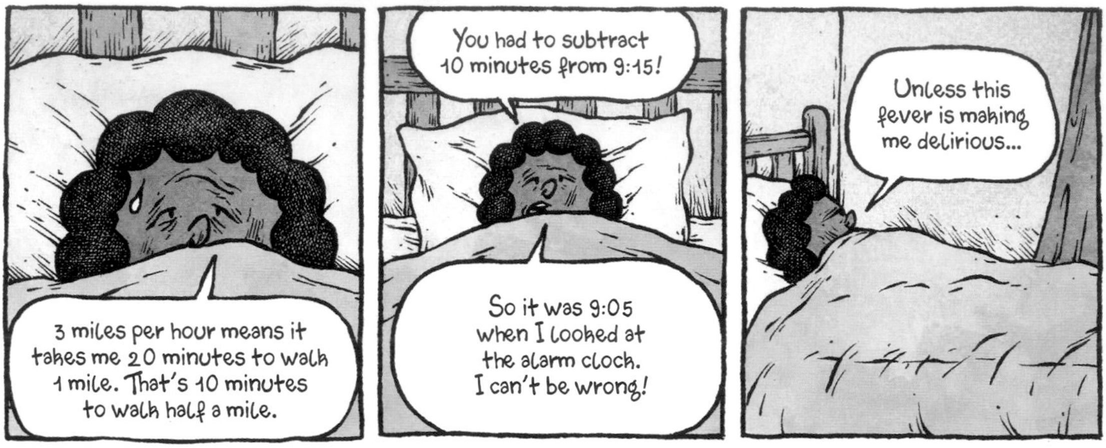
3 miles per hour means it takes me 20 minutes to walk 1 mile. That's 10 minutes to walk half a mile.
You had to subtract 10 minutes from 9:15!
So it was 9:05 when I looked at the alarm clock. I can't be wrong!
Unless this fever is making me delirious...

Solution : A+B+C+D+E...=?

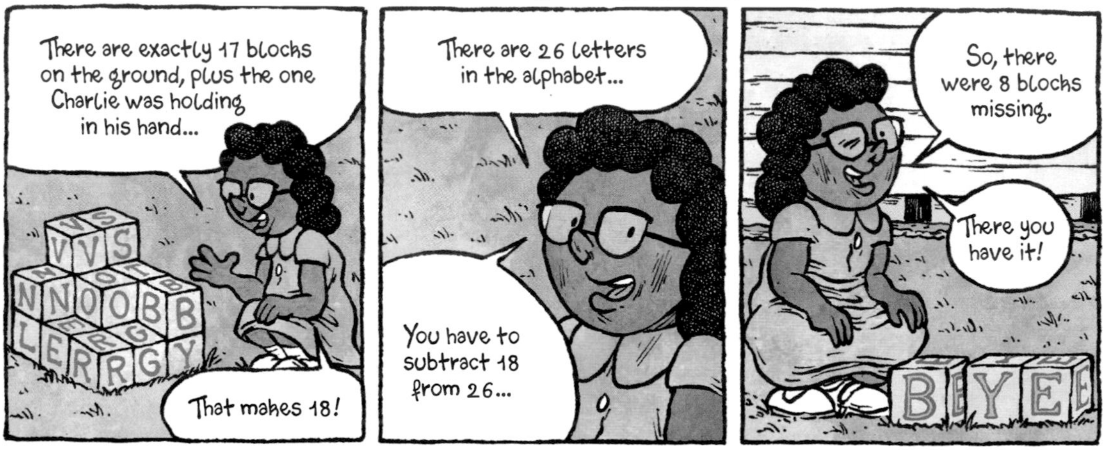
There are exactly 17 blocks on the ground, plus the one Charlie was holding in his hand...
That makes 18!
There are 26 letters in the alphabet...
You have to subtract 18 from 26...
So, there were 8 blocks missing.
There you have it!

Solution : 57

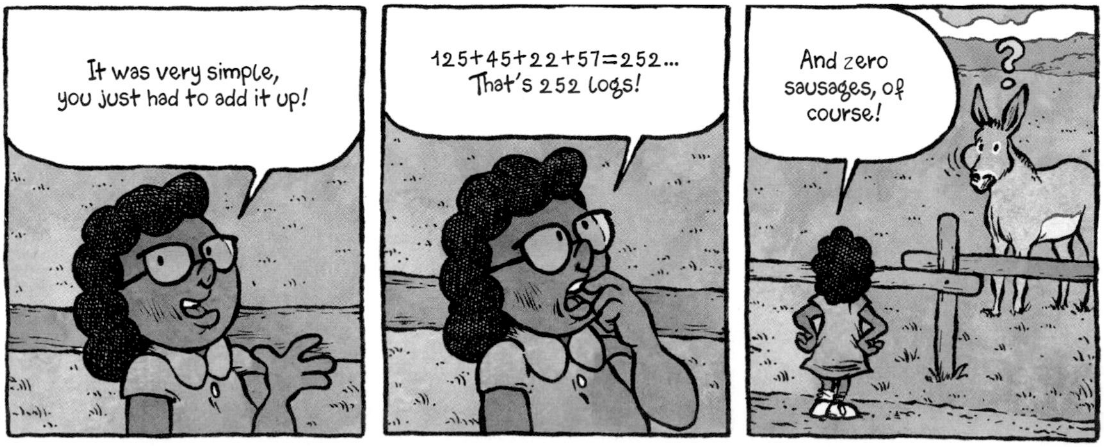
It was very simple, you just had to add it up!
125+45+22+57=252... That's 252 logs!
And zero sausages, of course!
?

Solution: 7

A multiple of 7 is a number in the 7 times table!

Ohhh, I see...

Well, there's 35, 42, and 49. But the only even number is...

...42?

Bingo!

Solution: 1, 2, 3

In the first sequence, you have to subtract 3 each time...

$54 - 3 = 51$
$51 - 3 = 48$
$48 - 3 = 45$
$45 - 3 = 42$
$42 - 3 = 39$

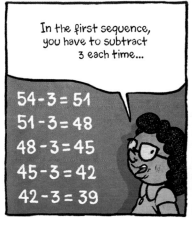

So the last number is 36!

$39 - 3 = 36$

In the second one, you need to multiply by 6!

$8 \times 6 = 48$
$48 \times 6 = 288$
$288 \times 6 = 1728$

The answer is 10,368!

$1728 \times 6 = 10368$

And finally, in the third one, you just have to multiply each number by itself...

$1 \times 1 = 1$
$2 \times 2 = 4$
$3 \times 3 = 9$
$4 \times 4 = 16$
$5 \times 5 = 25$

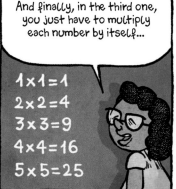

Which makes $8 \times 8 = 64$!

$6 \times 6 = 36$
$7 \times 7 = 49$
$8 \times 8 = 64$

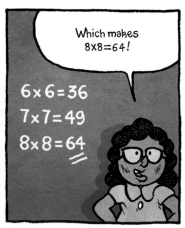

Solution: 4, 5, 6

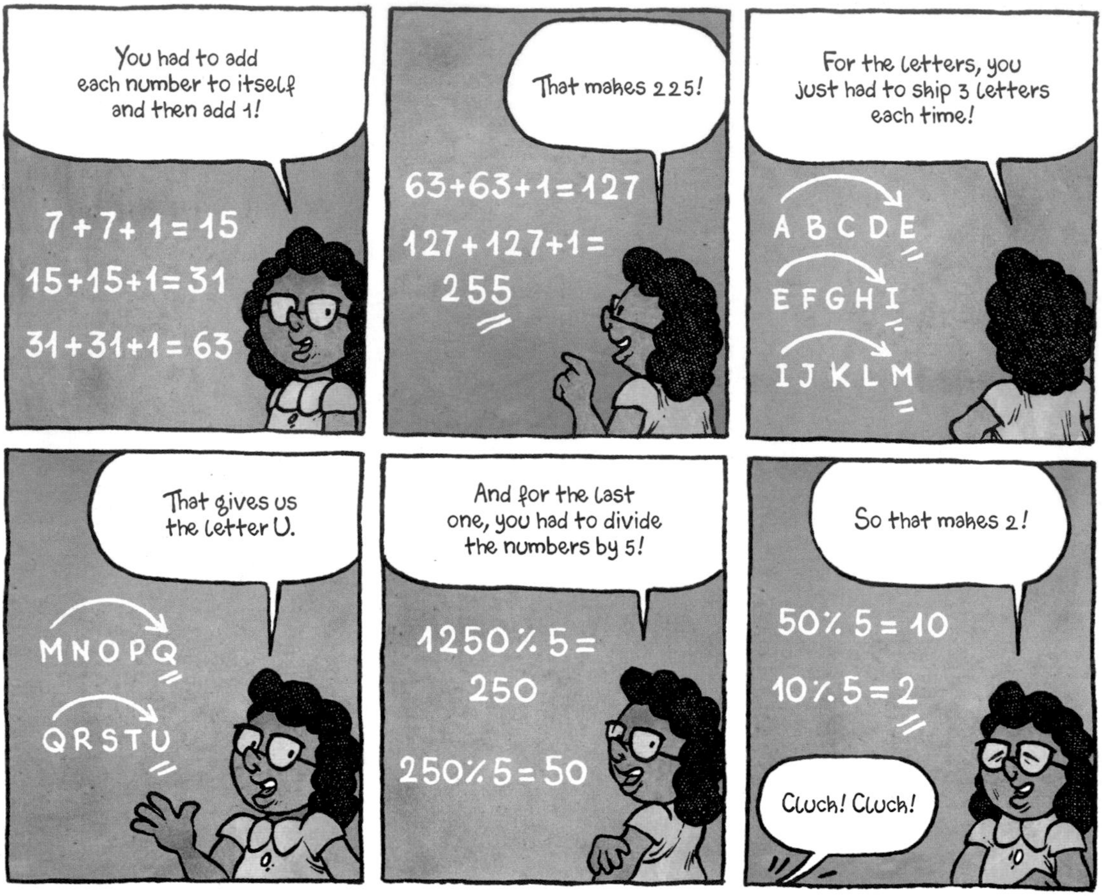

You had to add each number to itself and then add 1!
7 + 7 + 1 = 15
15 + 15 + 1 = 31
31 + 31 + 1 = 63
That makes 225!
63 + 63 + 1 = 127
127 + 127 + 1 =
255
For the letters, you just had to skip 3 letters each time!
A B C D E
E F G H I
I J K L M
That gives us the letter U.
M N O P Q
Q R S T U
And for the last one, you had to divide the numbers by 5!
1250 ÷ 5 =
250
250 ÷ 5 = 50
So that makes 2!
50 ÷ 5 = 10
10 ÷ 5 = 2
Cluck! Cluck!

Solution: 1 1/2 Hours

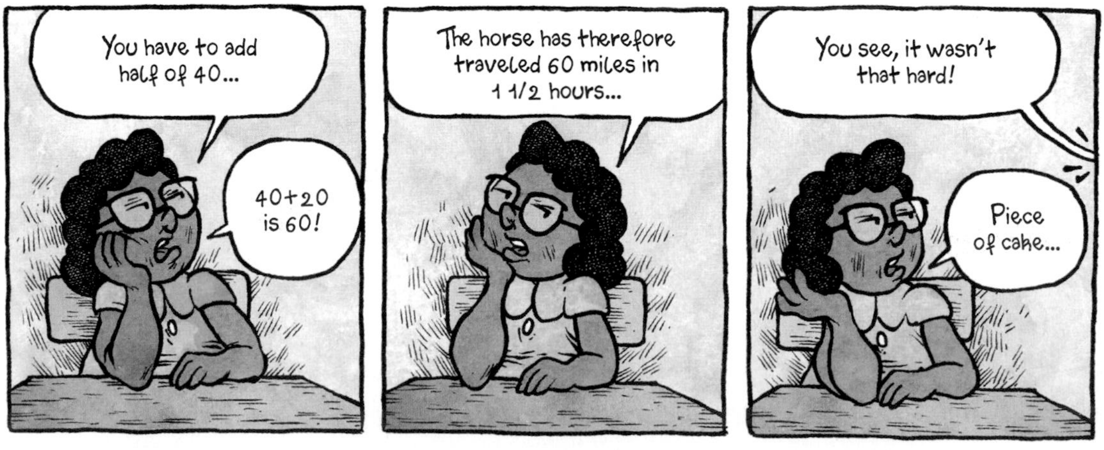

You have to add half of 40...
40+20 is 60!
The horse has therefore traveled 60 miles in 1 1/2 hours...
You see, it wasn't that hard!
Piece of cake...

Solution: 1.5 Quarts

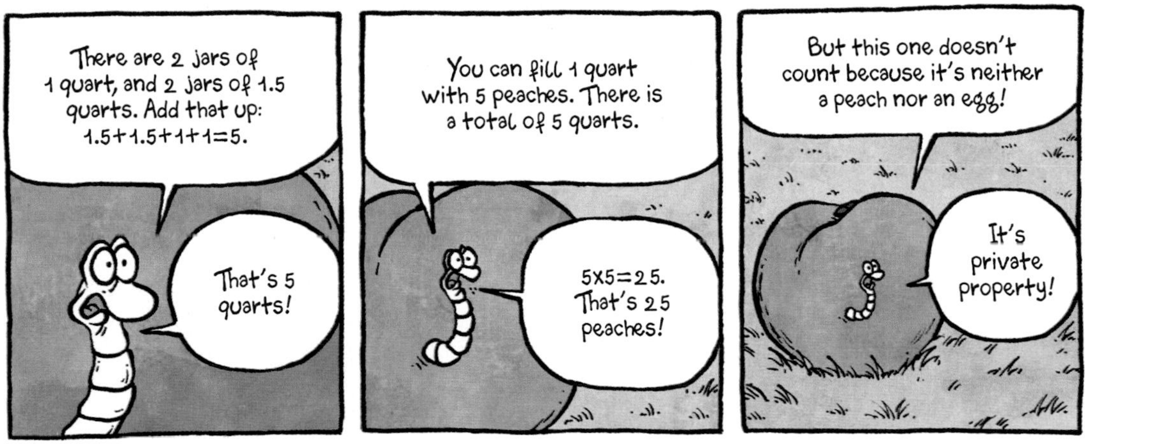
There are 2 jars of 1 quart, and 2 jars of 1.5 quarts. Add that up: 1.5+1.5+1+1=5.
That's 5 quarts!
You can fill 1 quart with 5 peaches. There is a total of 5 quarts.
5x5=25. That's 25 peaches!
But this one doesn't count because it's neither a peach nor an egg!
It's private property!

Solution: ÷4

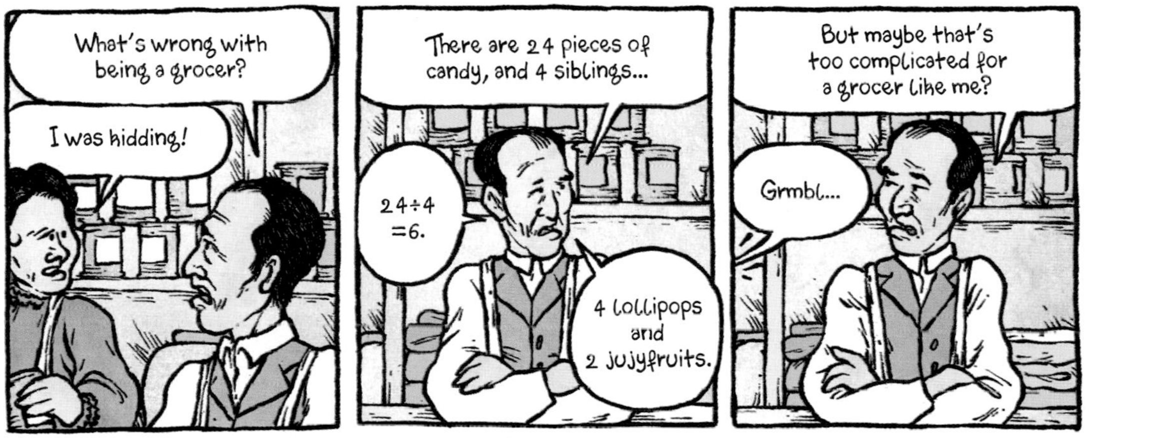
What's wrong with being a grocer?
I was kidding!
There are 24 pieces of candy, and 4 siblings...
24÷4 =6.
4 lollipops and 2 jujyfruits.
But maybe that's too complicated for a grocer like me?
Grmbl...

Solution: △

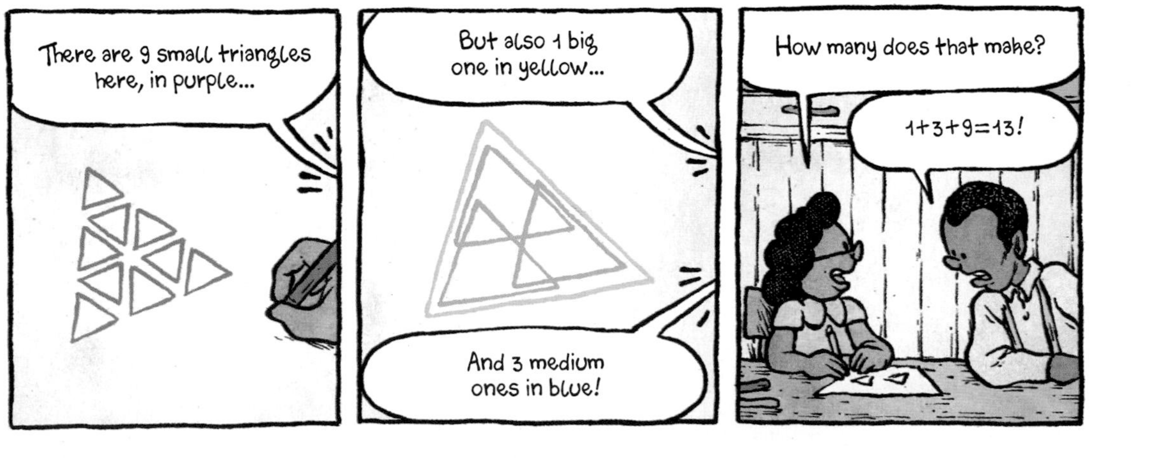
There are 9 small triangles here, in purple...
But also 1 big one in yellow...
And 3 medium ones in blue!
How many does that make?
1+3+9=13!

Solution: 1/3

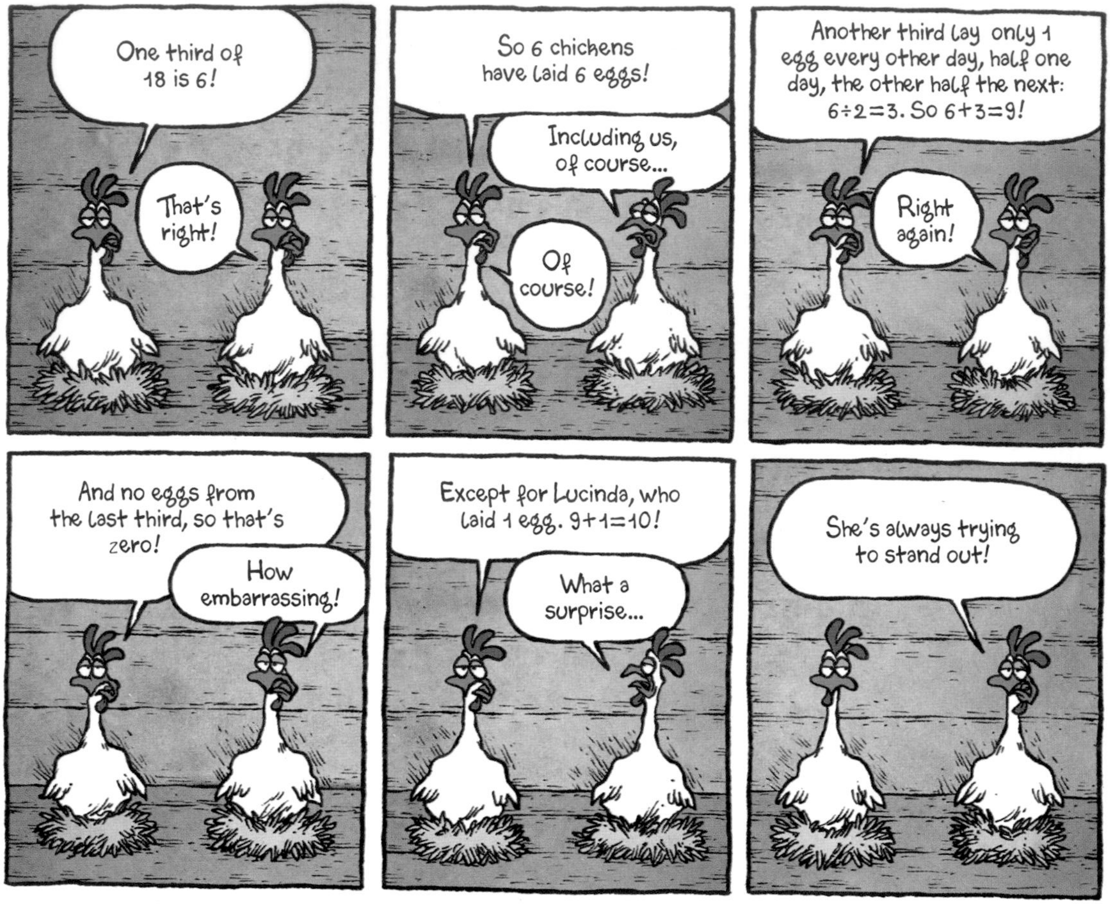
One third of 18 is 6!
That's right!
So 6 chickens have laid 6 eggs!
Including us, of course...
Of course!
Another third lay only 1 egg every other day, half one day, the other half the next: 6÷2=3. So 6+3=9!
Right again!
And no eggs from the last third, so that's zero!
How embarrassing!
Except for Lucinda, who laid 1 egg. 9+1=10!
What a surprise...
She's always trying to stand out!

Solution: 1/10,000

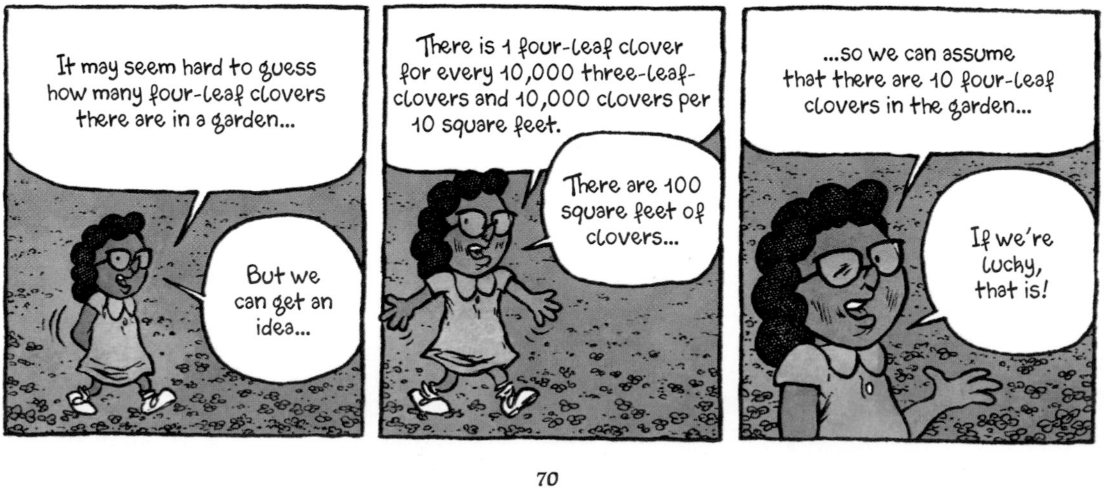
It may seem hard to guess how many four-leaf clovers there are in a garden...
But we can get an idea...
There is 1 four-leaf clover for every 10,000 three-leaf-clovers and 10,000 clovers per 10 square feet.
There are 100 square feet of clovers...
...so we can assume that there are 10 four-leaf clovers in the garden...
If we're lucky, that is!

Katherine's Workbook

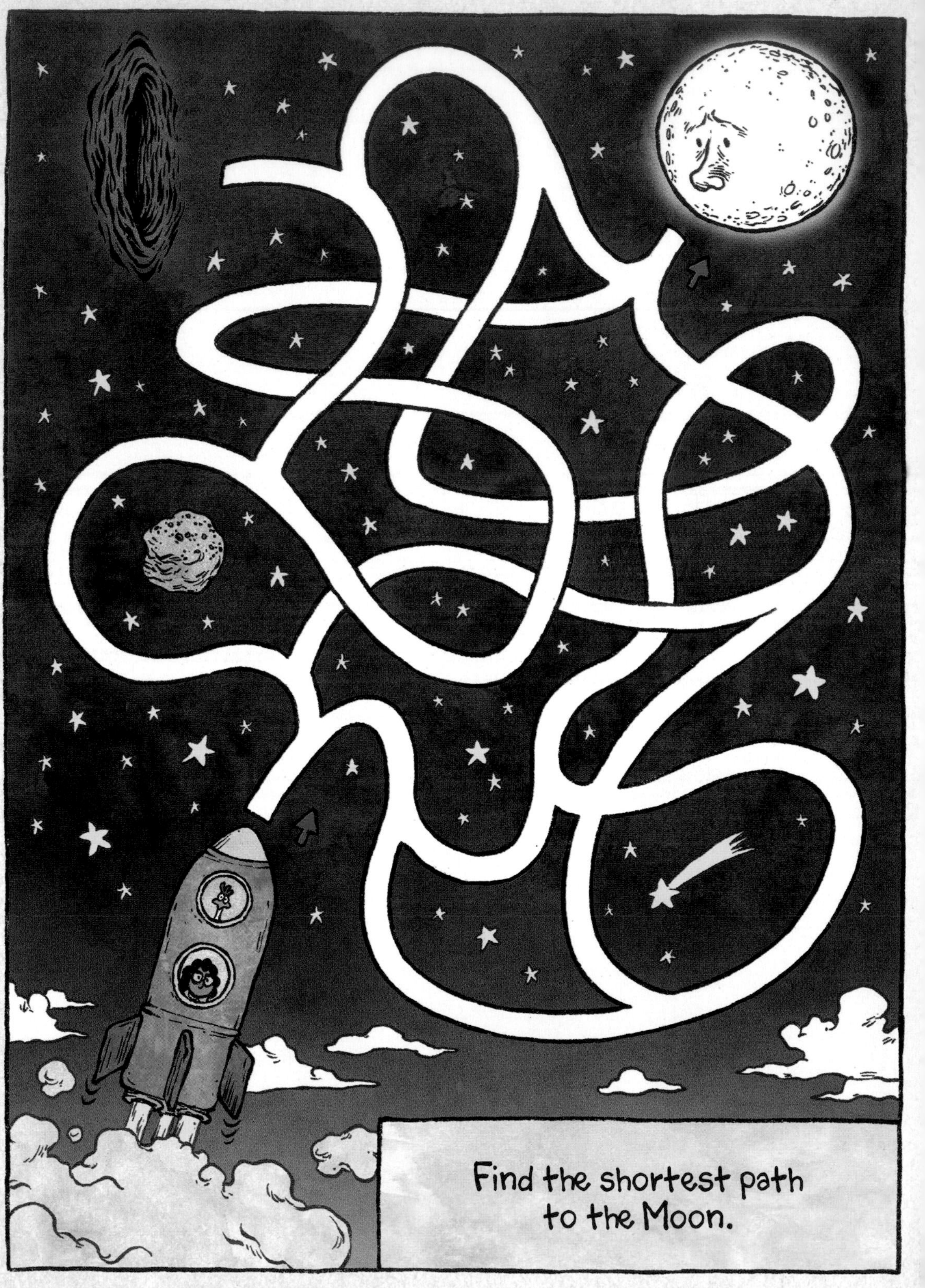
Find the shortest path
to the Moon.

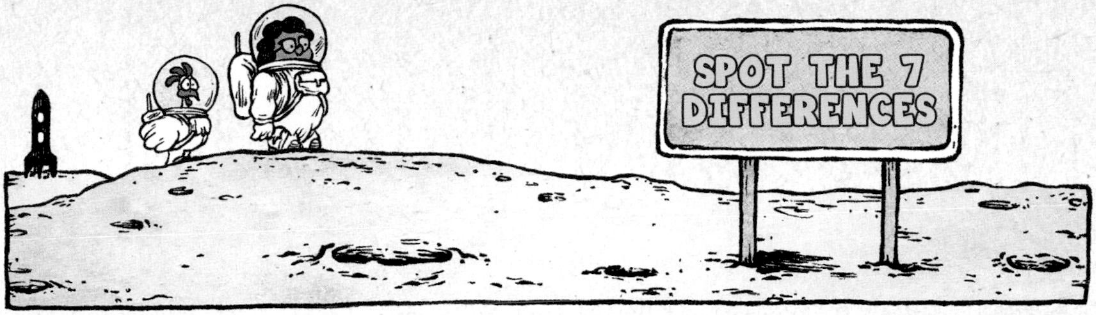
SPOT THE 7 DIFFERENCES

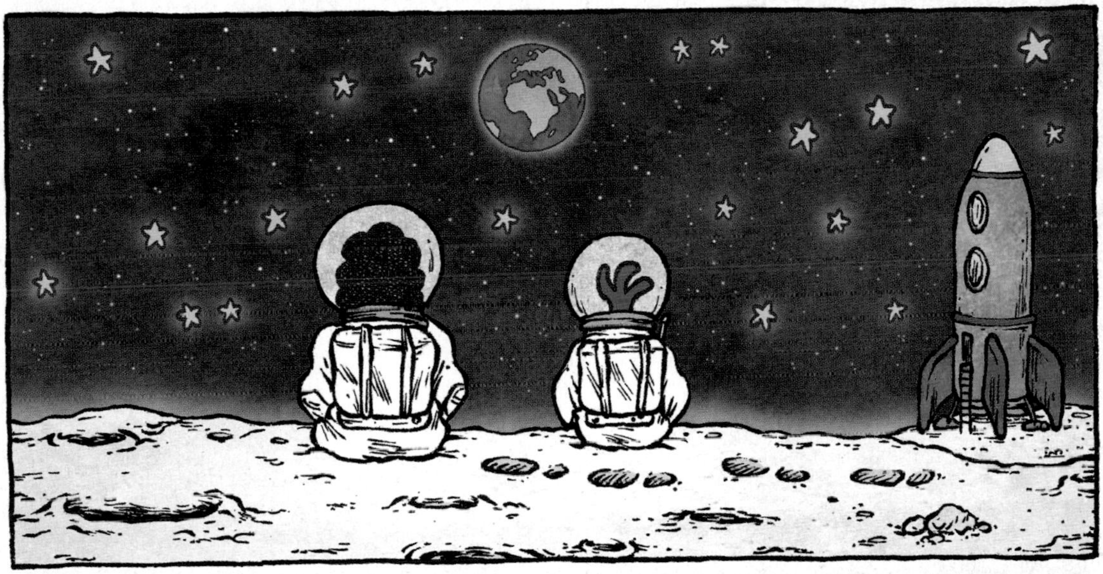

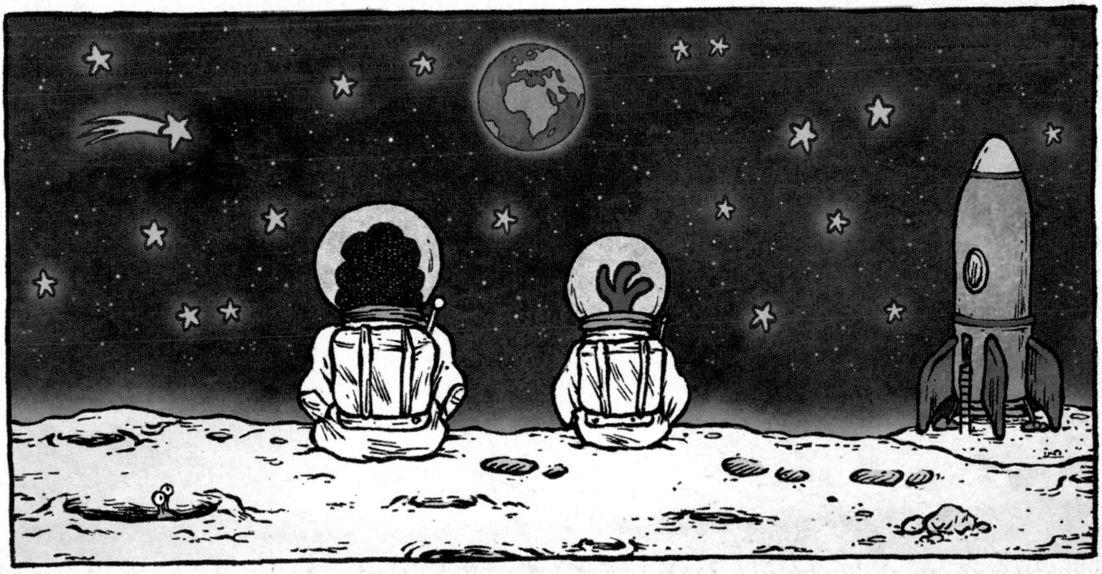

Solution

1. The star at the top right 2. The footprint 3. The shooting star 4. The color of the Earth 5. The critter in the crater 6. The spaceship window 7. The antenna on Katherine's suit.

Blast Off!

Why does the balloon shoot up like a rocket?

What you'll need:

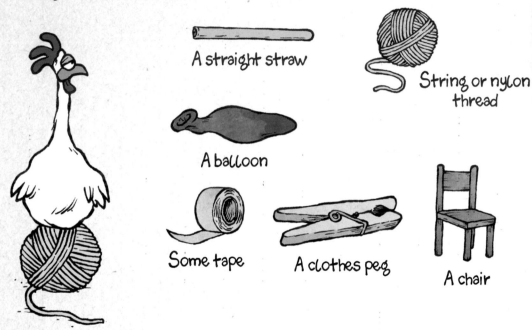

A straight straw

String or nylon thread

A balloon

Some tape

A clothes peg

A chair

The Experiment:

With the help of a grown up

1. Take a very thin piece of string and cut it 6 feet long. Put one end of the string through a straight straw that doesn't bend. Then tape the other end of the string to the back of a chair.

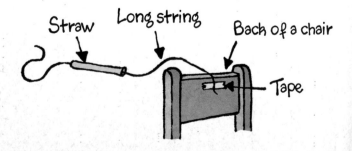

Straw   Long string   Back of a chair

Tape

2 Inflate a balloon as much as possible. Don't tie a knot! Use the clothes peg to close the open end and keep the air inside. Then, tape the balloon to the straw. Make sure the neck of the balloon is pointed towards the chair and parallel to the string.

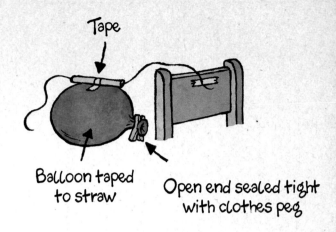

Tape

Balloon taped to straw

Open end sealed tight with clothes peg

3 Ask a grown-up to tape the other end of the string high up on a wall. The string should be taught. Release the clothes peg and...woosh! The balloon shoots up the string like a rocket!

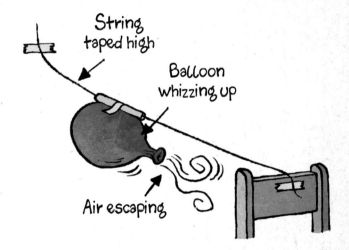

String taped high

Balloon whizzing up

Air escaping

How does it work?

When you blow, you force the air into the balloon. Inside, the air gets tight: it's "compressed," or "under pressure." When you release it, the air rushes out from one end, propelling the balloon in the other direction! It's called the law of action and reaction. Rocket engines also release compressed gas. Zoom! It thrusts the rocket forward, even through the vacuum of space!

Quiz

1 Approximately how many stars are there in the Milky Way?

a) 100
b) 100 million
c) 300 million
d) 100 billion

2 Which planet is sometimes called the Red Planet?

a) Mercury
b) Venus
c) Saturn
d) Mars

3 The Moon is:

a) a satellite
b) a planet
c) a star
d) an egg

4 How old is the Moon?

a) 3 years old
b) 163 years old
c) 1.3 million years old
d) 4.6 billion years old

5 What is the circumference of the Moon?

a) 2 miles
b) 123 miles
c) 6,783 miles
d) 189,971 miles

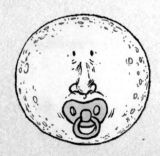

6 The Milky Way is:

    a) a planet
    b) a constellation
    c) a galaxy
    d) a yogurt

7 What is the distance between the Earth and the Moon?

    a) 14 miles
    b) 253 miles
    c) 238,855 miles
    d) 53,700,762 miles

8 What explosion is said to have created the universe?

    a) The Big Bang
    b) The Bling Bling
    c) The Bang Bang
    d) The Bada Boom

9 The craters on the Moon are caused by:

    a) ancient lakes
    b) meteorite impacts
    c) wells
    d) pimples

10 Which planet has visible rings?

    a) Earth
    b) Mars
    c) Saturn
    d) Mercury

Solution

1-c / 2-d / 3-a / 4-d / 5-c / 6-c / 7-c / 8-a / 9-b / 10-c

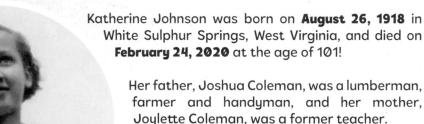

Katherine Johnson

© droits réservés

Katherine Johnson

Katherine Johnson was born on **August 26, 1918** in White Sulphur Springs, West Virginia, and died on **February 24, 2020** at the age of 101!

Her father, Joshua Coleman, was a lumberman, farmer and handyman, and her mother, Joylette Coleman, was a former teacher.

Gifted in mathematics, **she graduated high school at the** age of 14 and enrolled at **West Virginia University**. At the age of 18, she graduated not only with a degree in **mathematics,** but also in **French!**

© droits réservés

Joylette and Joshua Coleman, Katherine's parents, Margaret, her sister, Horace, her eldest brother, Katherine and Charlie, her middle brother.

In 1952, she started working for NASA as a **"human computer."** That's right, before the advent of calculating machines and electronic computers, computing was done by humans!

1,2,3...
12,13,14...

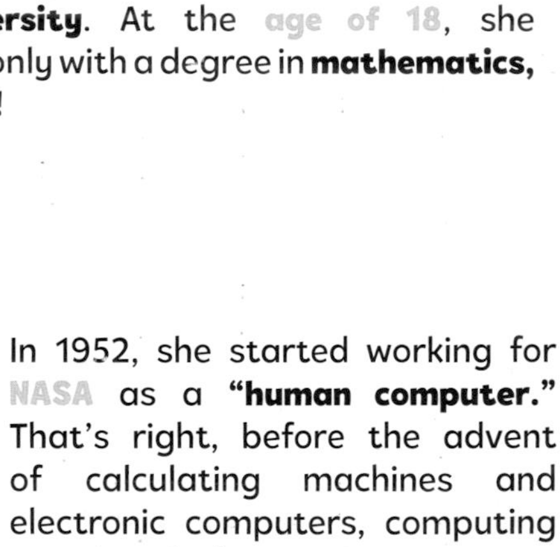

When she was temporarily assigned to the flight research team, her knowledge allowed her to quickly integrate into the team, made up of mostly white men. Katherine said she ignored the racial and gender barriers that were still present and even asked to participate in meetings where no women had previously been included.

In 1958, she started doing trajectory analysis for spacecraft launches. Her calculations were so accurate that in 1962, astronaut John Glenn asked for her specifically to verify computer calculations.

In 1969, she was on the team tasked with calculating the trajectory of the Apollo Lunar Module's ascent from the surface of the Moon.

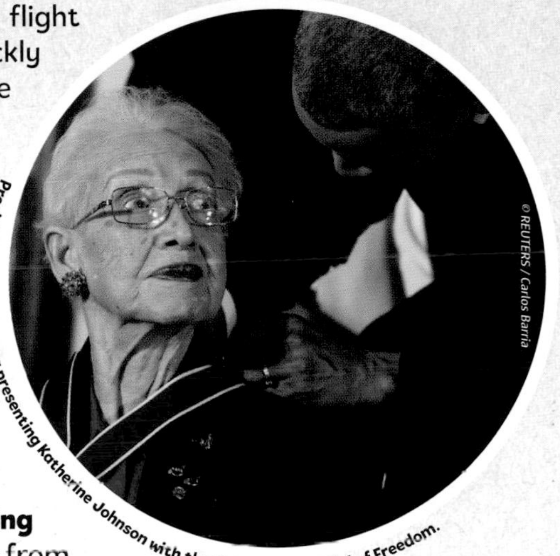
© REUTERS / Carlos Barria
President Barack Obama presenting Katherine Johnson with the Presidential Medal of Freedom.

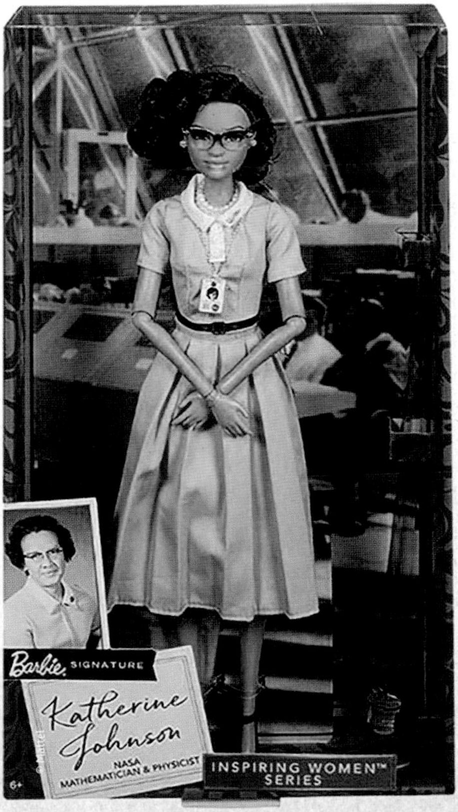
Barbie SIGNATURE
Katherine Johnson
NASA MATHEMATICIAN & PHYSICIST
INSPIRING WOMEN™ SERIES
6+

Katherine Johnson is a legend in the history of science and the conquest of space and was presented with many awards, such as the Presidential Medal of Freedom and the Congressional Gold Medal – **the two highest civilian awards in the United States** – and the Silver Snoopy Award, which honors **NASA's most outstanding employees...**

She was also a pioneer in promoting African-American history. In 2016, author Margot Lee Shetterly chronicled Johnson's career in her book *Hidden Figures: The American Dream and the Untold Story of the Black Women Who Helped Win the Space Race*, which was then adapted into a film that same year. Two years later, the makers of the world-famous **Barbie doll even announced a doll in her likeness** as part of its collection dedicated to inspiring women!

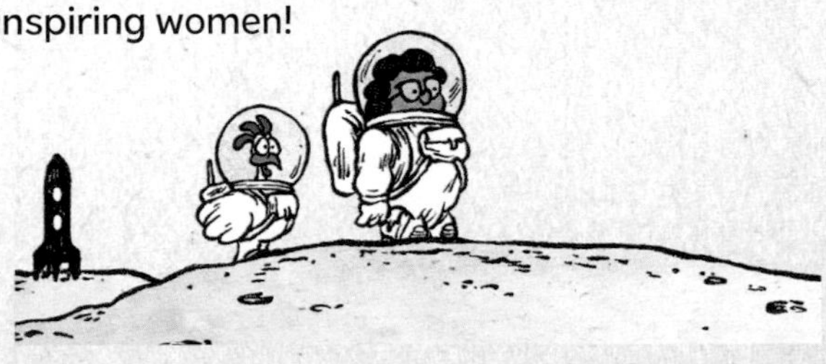

TEACHING GUIDE

Young
KATHERINE JOHNSON
Augel
24
x 63
1512
BiG

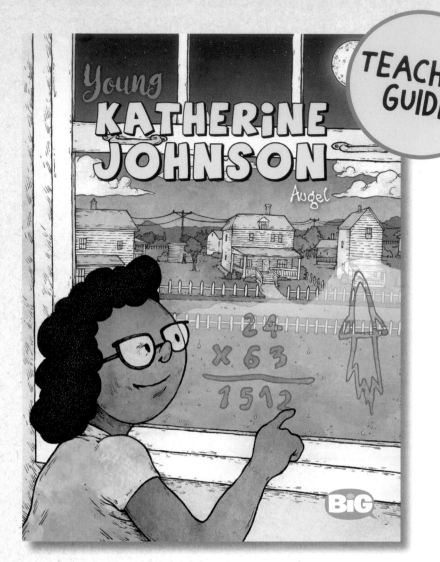

OVERVIEW

How many stars are in the sky? What is the Moon's circumference? How many numbers can you use to describe a lion? These are just some of the mathematical questions in *Young Katherine Johnson's* mind—the same Katherine Johnson that would grow up to be one of NASA's "Human Computers" and break down barriers for Black women in America.

In *Young Katherine Johnson*, writer and artist William Augel explores what the mind of the Presidential Medal of Freedom winner might have been like as a child growing up on her family's farm home in White Sulfur Springs, West Virginia. Katherine sees the world differently than others, mostly through the lens of numbers and equations that she believes can explain anything. Her talents and curiosity drive her, but they also drive others crazy! Follow Katherine through short, entertaining vignettes as she calculates her way through her early life, and explores things that cannot be explained with numbers, like her identity, her relationships, and her dreams.

CHARACTERS

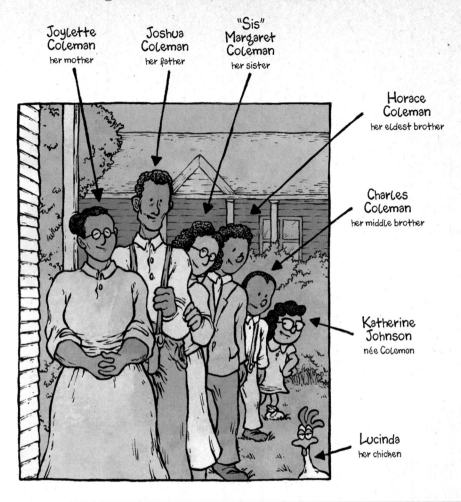

Joylette Coleman
her mother

Joshua Coleman
her father

"Sis" Margaret Coleman
her sister

Horace Coleman
her eldest brother

Charles Coleman
her middle brother

Katherine Johnson
née Coleman

Lucinda
her chicken

Katherine The protagonist in most vignettes in Young Katherine Johnson. Katherine is smart, witty, and unquenchably curious about the world around her. She loves school and learning, and she will find numbers and equations in any situation. She revels in solving problems using math and encouraging others to see the world through her numerical perspective.

Katherine's Parents Katherine's parents appear in many of the vignettes throughout the book. Katherine's father, Joshua, works the family's farm in addition to working many other jobs throughout White Sulfur Springs. Katherine's Mother, Joylette, tends to many of the domestic duties. Both parents nurture Katherine's curiosity, mentoring and comforting her as she learns to navigates her world.

Katherine's Siblings Katherine's three older siblings—Margaret, Horace, and Charles—are constantly bewildered by their youngest sister. They often struggle to understand Katherine's perspective but love and support her as best as they can—with a healthy dose of teasing and rivalry. Katherine spends the most time with Charles, pondering facts about the world and space, and—to Charles' chagrin—eventually sharing a school classroom.

Lucinda Katherine's family owns many chickens, but Lucinda is Katherine's favorite. Lucinda struggles to lay eggs of her own, but she desperately seeks to brood as many egg-shaped objects as possible.

The Moon In Katherine's dreams, she often visits an anthropomorphized Moon, asking her questions about her surface, gravity, and space. These visits usually result in Katherine being suddenly awoken, having fallen off of her bed while dreaming.

THEMES

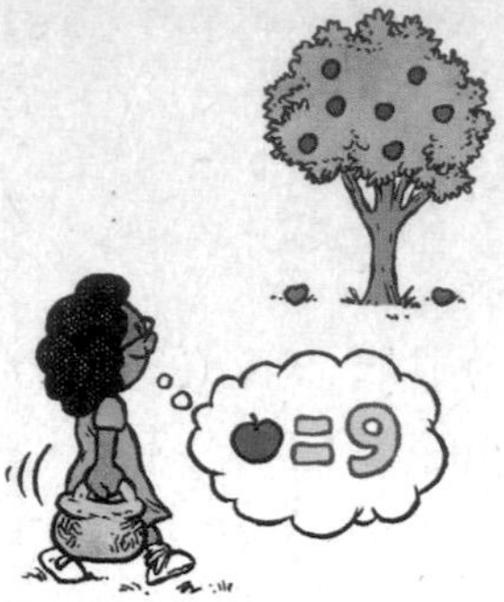
=9

Math is All Around Us Everywhere Katherine looks she sees numbers and equations. From the amount of time it will take her to get to school to the amount of candy she gets to share with her siblings, Katherine excels at navigating the world using math. She finds comfort knowing that the world can be distilled down and explained with numbers! Katherine shows others—and the reader—many of the ways that math is useful in our daily lives and beyond.

Black Identity Before Katherine was one of the few Black scientists working at NASA in the mid 20th century she began exploring her identity as a child in White Sulfur Springs. In multiple vignettes Katherine and her siblings grapple with how their experiences differ from their White neighbors'. From not being able to use the local skating rink to not knowing what "relaxing" means to contemplating what her social status would be if lunar aliens enslaved White people, Katherine's identity as a Black woman prominently shapes her worldview and her role in it—possibly even influencing her comfort in the objective truth of numbers.

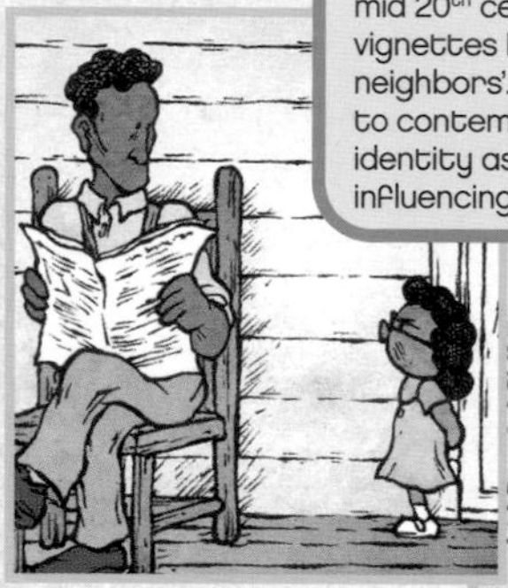

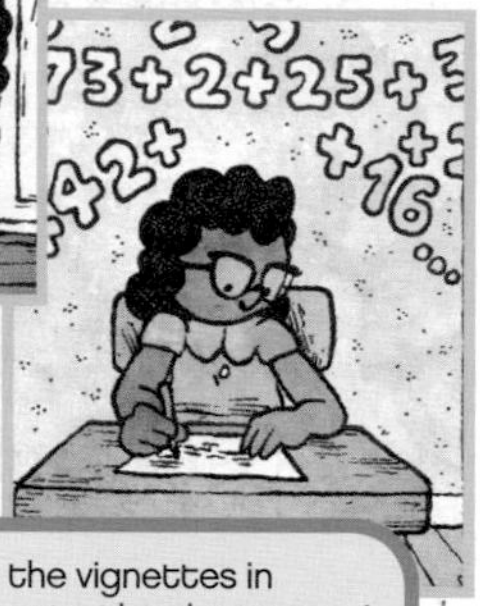

Giftedness/Being Different Katherine's natural gifts for math set her apart from her family and peers, and they often cause her to see the world differently than others. Her talents are like superpowers, allowing her to see and calculate the numbers in any situation. Her family and teachers, however, don't always understand Katherine's way of thinking and can struggle to relate. This sometimes causes them frustration, confusion, or exasperation, even though Katherine is clearly gifted.

Astronomy Before Katherine worked for NASA she dreamt of the Moon! Katherine has a natural curiosity of the Moon and beyond. She counts the stars, explains constellations to her sister, and even ponders the idea of lunar aliens with her brother. In her dreams, Katherine visits the Moon, asking her as many questions as she can before being brought back to reality.

Different Perspectives Many of the vignettes in *Young Katherine Johnson* illustrate the characters' different perspectives on various subjects. Katherine's perspective on the world almost always involves numbers. Her sister might view a math textbook as mundane, but Katherine sees it as a thrilling bedtime story. Katherine's brothers see a ball to play with, whereas Lucinda the chicken sees it as an egg to be brooded. And Katherine's family sees the world through the lens of a Black family in the early 20th century, far different from their White neighbors.

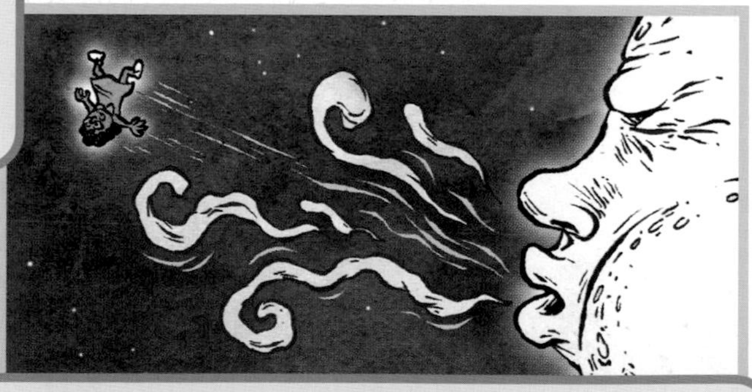

SETTINGS

Katherine's Home Many of the vignettes in Young Katherine Johnson take place at her family's farm home in White Sulfur Springs, West Virginia. Her home is place for learning, exploration, contemplation, and countless numbers and equations.

White Sulfur Springs, West Virginia Katherine's town takes its name from a sulfur water source located at The Greenbrier, a local country club. Katherine learns about her identity by the way her family members relate to the other townsfolk. The local grocery, Katherine's school, and much of her father's business all reside in town.

Katherine's School A few vignettes in *Young Katherine Johnson* take place in her school where Katherine excels and often perplexes her teachers. Eventually, Katherine is advanced beyond her grade level and moves to join her older brother, Charles, in his classes.

Outer Space/The Moon In Katherine's dreams, she visits the Moon to have discussions about its nature and properties. Inevitably, Katherine returns to the real world with a crash as she falls out of her bed.

PRE-READING ACTIVITIES

What's Your Perspective? Much of Katherine's world is colored by her love for numbers and equations. In this activity, students will prepare to read Young Katherine Johnson by exploring their own passions and how they might impact their worldview.

- First, give students a blank piece of paper and ask students to split their paper into four quadrants.

- Next, instruct students to draw the following, one in each quadrant.
  1. A window
  2. A book
  3. A tablet, phone, or TV screen
  4. A t-shirt

  For each picture, instruct students to include their own details. For example, what can the students see through the window? What is on the cover of the book? What is on the screen? What is on the t-shirt?

- Next, ask each student to pass their paper to a peer. Have the peer study their paper. Then, each student should try to guess their peer's passions or special skills based on the drawings they receive.

- Finally, facilitate a class discussion in which you examine how our passions and skills shape our perspectives of the world. Often, we see our passions in places that others do not. Many of us may see the world in relation to our favorite video games, or a sport that we love, or stories to be told. People with different passions and skills might see the world in a different way!

I Spy - Math! In *Young Katherine Johnson*, Katherine sees numbers and equations all around her. In this activity, students will prepare to read the book by spotting hidden math equations all around them.

- First, explain to students that math is everywhere they look! Give them one or two examples, such as calculating how many pairs of shoes are in the classroom, or the area of the white board.

- Next, give students time to explore the classroom looking for hidden math problems. Examples that students might find: volume of a text book, the amount of books on a bookshelf, the amount of food a class pet needs per week or amount of tiles in the ceiling.

- After exploring, ask each student to represent a math problem they found on paper using drawings and equations. If students struggle to find a math problem or represent it, more teacher examples can be given for the students to emulate.

- Ask students to form small groups and have each student share their equation with the rest of the group. Students can work together to verify each other's visual and numerical representations.

- Finally, ask each group to identify their favorite hidden equation. This can be shared with the rest of the class.

Dreams of the Impossible In *Young Katherine Johnson*, Katherine often dreams of the Moon, and even discusses with her brother how humans could travel there. Later in life, the real Katherine Johnson would become a NASA Scientist, helping with calculations for lunar missions. In this activity, students will prepare to read the book by dreaming of something impossible that they might someday like to achieve through science or math.

- First, prepare students by discussing that not too long ago, space travel and lunar landings were thought to be impossible. Through science, humans were able to land on the Moon in 1969, and we now have advanced satellites, rovers, and images of Space! Images from the lunar landing and the new James Webb telescope can be used for reference.

- Next, ask students to think of something that is currently deemed impossible but could theoretically be achieved someday through scientific research and discovery!

- Have students share and discuss their ideas in small groups. What makes their idea impossible? Why do they want to make this impossible feat a reality? How might this advancement help humankind?

- Finally, conclude the class discussion by linking their ideas back to science, math, and space travel. Remind students that the scientists who achieved these discoveries were once kids that dreamed of the impossible, just like them! Students can then read the short biography of Katherine Johnson located in the back of the book before continuing to read the rest of the graphic novel.

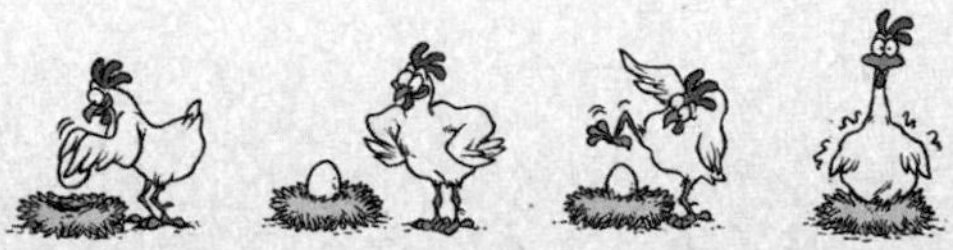

DISCUSSION QUESTIONS

• How did being Black affect Katherine's life as a child? How might her life have been different if she was White? Do you think this affects her love of math and numbers? Why or why not?

• What do you think Katherine means in "7000" when she says that mathematics is "the only universal language"? How is math similar to spoken languages? How is it different? How can a universal language help you navigate the world?

• Why do you think Katherine likes math so much? What in the images or text makes you think this?

• In "142," Katherine asks her father what it means to relax. When her father tells her it means to "not doing anything," Katherine replies, "We're allowed to do that?" Why do you think Katherine replies this way? Do you think it is easy or enjoyable for her to relax? Why or why not? Why does Katherine's father never get to relax? What does relaxing mean to you? How often do you relax, and do you enjoy it? Why or why not?

• In "X=Y," Katherine says that everything can be explained with math, then says "Otherwise, the world would be a scary place!" Why does Katherine think this? Do you agree with Kathrine? Why or why not?

• What are some ways that Katherine's father uses math to do his job?

• What is Charles and Katherine's relationship like? How does Charles feel about Katherine, and how does Katherine feel about Charles? What in the images or text tells you this?

• In "48,000," why does Katherine say "poor chickens" when thinking about carnivores and herbivores? Why does she say that an elephant can eat 15,000 lbs of food in a month, but 14,000 in February?

• How do the images in "6,786" help you understand what is happening in the vignette? Why does the Moon ask, "Have you ever had the same dream over and over again"? Based on the clues in the image and text, what do you think circumference or perimeter mean?

• What does Katherine's teacher think of her questions in "1 ½ Hours"? What in the text makes you think that? Why is Katherine asking so many questions about the horse?

• What do you think "pretentious" means as used in "7"? Why do you think that?

• In "H2O," Katherine quotes a Chinese proverb that says, "When the wise man points at the Moon, the fool looks at the finger." What do you think this means?

• What is the story "24" showing the reader? How do you know this without any text?

• After reading the book, how would you describe young Katherine's personality? Based on the comic, what do you think her friends and family think about her?

• After reading the book, how would you describe Katherine's view of the world? Why do you think she views the world this way? Does she view it similarly or differently than other people?

• Do you think the world would be a better place if everyone viewed it the same way or differently? Why do you think this? What evidence from the text or images supports your thinking?

• How does Katherine's view of the world affect her relationships with others?

• How would you describe Lucinda the chicken's worldview? How does that affect how she interacts with the world?

• What are some of the themes in Young Katherine Johnson? Support your answer with evidence from the comic.

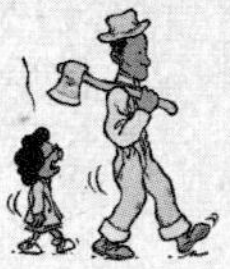

PROJECT IDEAS

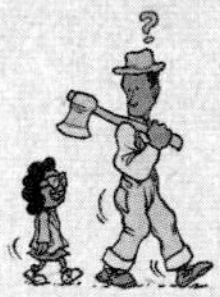

Math Comic *Young Katherine Johnson* features multiple word problems in a comic format. In this project, using the solvable problems in the book as a model, students will create their own one-page comic with two or more characters that presents the reader with a math problem. If students completed the "I Spy – Math!" pre-reading activity, they may use those findings as a start for this project.

- First, tell students that they will be making their own one-page comic that presents the reader with a math word problem, similar to what they read in Young Katherine Johnson. Instruct students to come up with a setting and 2-3 characters to feature in their comic. The characters could be real people, established fictional characters, or characters of the students' own creation. Settings could be fictional or reality-based.
- Next, instruct students to think of a problem that might exist within the setting of their comic. Encourage students to be creative and original when coming up with their problems. If students struggle to come up with ideas, however, instruct them to refer to the math problems in Young Katherine Johnson for inspiration.
- Instruct students to create a rough draft of their comic using only pencil and including speech bubbles, backgrounds, etc. The teacher should review students' drafts and provide feedback before lettings students color their final comics.
- When comics are completed, encourage students to do a gallery walk and view other students' work. Students can use sticky notes to leave positive feedback on other students' comics.

Young Geniuses In *Young Katherine Johnson*, the author imagines what ordinary moments in Katherine Johnson's childhood might have been like based on what we know about her adult life and her legacy. While the stories told are not necessarily factual, they provide a humorous look into Katherine's personality and possible inspirations. In this project, students will create a similar Young Genius story based on a prominent figure from history or pop culture.

- First, instruct students to choose a prominent figure from history or pop culture that they would like to learn more about. If desired, teachers can provide their students selections to choose from.
- Next, instruct students to research their figure using age-appropriate books from the school library or guided internet research. Instruct students to make notes of their chosen figure's personality and notable accomplishments.
- Ask students to brainstorm what their chosen figure might have been like as a child. What childhood events could have inspired their adult accomplishments? What might their personality traits have been as a child?
- Finally, asks students to create a short story, series of vignettes, journal entries, play, YouTube sketch, comic, or other portrayal of their chosen figure that brings these imagined stories to life.

Character Creation Discovery In *Young Katherine Johnson*, Katherine dreams of the Moon and asks her many questions to fulfill her curiosity. The Moon, however, is often cheeky and enigmatic! In this project, students will create an anthropomorphized character based on an object they want to learn more about, then they will bring it to life through facts gained from research.

- First, ask students to think of an object that seems mysterious to them that they would like to learn more about. If desired, teachers can give students selections to choose from, such as planets in our solar system or technological innovations.
- Next, instruct students to brainstorm 4-6 questions they have about that object.
- Ask students to research that object using age-appropriate books from the school library or guided internet research. Students should document answers to the questions they brainstormed earlier, as well as any other interesting facts they discover.
- Next, tell students to imagine their object as an anthropomorphized character and have them brainstorm character traits based on facts from their research. Teachers may want to have thought of their own example ahead of time to demonstrate how facts can be turned into character traits. For example, a cold planet might not be very friendly and speak with shivers in their voice, a lightbulb might be very smart, or a game controller might speak in video game lingo.
- Finally, have students write out a simulated conversation between themselves and their new character where the students' questions are answered. This can be written in the form of a script, a short story, or a comic. Students' chosen objects should embody the specified character traits when they speak.

PROJECT IDEAS (CONT.)

Creating Your Classroom Katherine Johnson used numbers and equations to help her solve problems and envision her dreams, such as space travel, fulfilled! Many architects and designers use numbers in similar ways. In this project, students will become designers and use math to create a scaled 2D floorplan of their ideal classroom.

- First, tell students that they will use math and numbers to imagine new possibilities, just like Katherine Johnson did when she helped get rockets and astronauts to and from the Moon! Tell students that they will be imagining and designing a floor plan for their perfect classroom. Teachers can show examples of real-life floor plans to give students an idea of what they will be creating.

- Next, allow students to work in groups to measure the physical features of the classroom that cannot be changed: perimeter, door size, support structures, etc. Have students record their findings.

- Next, using graph paper on a document camera or smart board, model calculating and drawing at scale by working with the class to calculate and draw a floor plan of the classroom's walls, doors, support structures, etc. Students may follow along to create their own floor plan.

- After creating the basic floor plan, the teacher can model adding elements to create their own ideal classroom. The teacher can insert practical elements (such as desks and chairs) and fun or silly elements (such as an ice cream machine or arcade cabinet) to their floor plan. As the teacher is adding elements, they can have the class help them calculate and draw scaled measurements.

- Allow students to brainstorm and draw their own scaled floor plans of their ideal classrooms. Each element of their floorplans should be labeled. Separately, students should list out the various added elements of their classroom and their "real" dimensions. Depending on teachers' scope for the project, they may also have students write out equations used to translate their "real" dimensions to their scaled dimensions, or require students to include the area of each added element.

- Finally, have students present their floorplans to the class, explaining each element they chose to put in their classroom and why they chose to do so.

FURTHER PAIRINGS

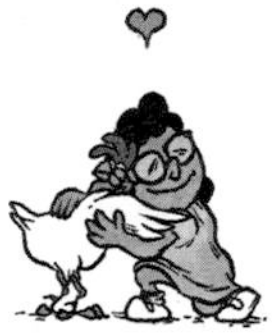

Young Mozart by William Augel. Humanoids, 2019 (Graphic novel)

Young Leonardo by William Augel. Humanoids, 2021 (Graphic novel)

Young Agatha Christie by William Augel. Humanoids, 2022 (Graphic novel)

Ghosts of Science Past by Joseph Sieracki and Jesse Lonegran. Humanoids, 2022 (Graphic novel)

Hidden Figures directed by Theodore Melfi. 20th Century Fox, 2016 (Film)

October Sky directed by Joe Johnston. Universal Pictures, 1998 (Film)

Hidden Figures by Margot Lee Shetterly, Winifred Conkling, and Laura Freeman. HarperCollins, 2018 (Book)

The Story of Katherine Johnson: A Biography Book for New Readers by Andrea Thorpe. Rockridge Press, 2021 (Book)

Reaching for the Moon: The Autobiography of NASA Mathematician Katherine Johnson by Katherine Johnson. Atheneum Books for Young Readers, 2020 (Autobiography)

NASA star Katherine Johnson Blazed a Path for #Blackgirlmagic by Duchess Harris. The Washington Post, 2020. https://newsela.com/read/lib-katherine-johnson-blackgirlmagic/id/2001006155/ (News article)

The Magic School Bus: Math Explosion. Young Scientist Club, 2014 (Board game)

Outnumbered: Improbable Heroes. Genius Games, 2021 (Board game)

Kerbal Space Program. Squad, 2015 (Video game)

The reading of this graphic novel in combination with a thoughtful analysis through writing, presentation, or discussion (such as the projects and discussion questions within this guide), can promote the teaching or reinforcement of the following 3rd and 4th grade Reading: Literature and Math Common Core Standards, as well as various Reading: Foundational Skills, Writing, History/Social Studies, and Speaking & Listening Common Core Standards.

GRADE 3 MATH

CCSS.MATH.CONTENT.3.OA.A.1
Interpret products of whole numbers, e.g., interpret 5 × 7 as the total number of objects in 5 groups of 7 objects each.

CCSS.MATH.CONTENT.3.OA.A.2
Interpret whole-number quotients of whole numbers, e.g., interpret 56 · 8 as the number of objects in each share when 56 objects are partitioned equally into 8 shares, or as a number of shares when 56 objects are partitioned into equal shares of 8 objects each.

CCSS.MATH.CONTENT.3.OA.A.3
Use multiplication and division within 100 to solve word problems in situations involving equal groups, arrays, and measurement quantities, e.g., by using drawings and equations with a symbol for the unknown number to represent the problem.

CCSS.MATH.CONTENT.3.OA.A.4
Determine the unknown whole number in a multiplication or division equation relating three whole numbers.

CCSS.MATH.CONTENT.3.OA.C.7
Fluently multiply and divide within 100, using strategies such as the relationship between multiplication and division (e.g., knowing that 8 × 5 = 40, one knows 40 · 5 = 8) or properties of operations. By the end of Grade 3, know from memory all products of two one-digit numbers.

CCSS.MATH.CONTENT.3.OA.D.8
Solve two-step word problems using the four operations. Represent these problems using equations with a letter standing for the unknown quantity. Assess the reasonableness of answers using mental computation and estimation strategies including rounding.

CCSS.MATH.CONTENT.3.NBT.A.2
Fluently add and subtract within 1000 using strategies and algorithms based on place value, properties of operations, and/or the relationship between addition and subtraction.

CCSS.MATH.CONTENT.3.MD.A.1
Tell and write time to the nearest minute and measure time intervals in minutes, Solve word problems involving addition and subtraction of time intervals in minutes, e.g., by representing the problem on a number line diagram.

CCSS.MATH.CONTENT.3.MD.A.2
Measure and estimate liquid volumes and masses of objects using standard units of grams (g), kilograms (kg), and liters (l).1 Add, subtract, multiply, or divide to solve one-step word problems involving masses or volumes that are given in the same units, e.g., by using drawings (such as a beaker with a measurement scale) to represent the problem.2

GRADE 3 READING: LITERATURE

CCSS.ELA-LITERACY.RL.3.1 Ask and answer questions to demonstrate understanding of a text, referring explicitly to the text as the basis for the answers.

CCSS.ELA-LITERACY.RL.3.3 Describe characters in a story (e.g., their traits, motivations, or feelings) and explain how their actions contribute to the sequence of events

CCSS.ELA-LITERACY.RL.3.4 Determine the meaning of words and phrases as they are used in a text, distinguishing literal from nonliteral language.

CCSS.ELA-LITERACY.RL.3.5 Refer to parts of stories, dramas, and poems when writing or speaking about a text, using terms such as chapter, scene, and stanza; describe how each successive part builds on earlier sections.

CCSS.ELA-LITERACY.RL.3.6 Distinguish their own point of view from that of the narrator or those of the characters.

CCSS.ELA-LITERACY.RL.3.7 Explain how specific aspects of a text's illustrations contribute to what is conveyed by the words in a story (e.g., create mood, emphasize aspects of a character or setting)

CCSS.ELA-LITERACY.RL.3.10 By the end of the year, read and comprehend literature, including stories, dramas, and poetry, at the high end of the grades 2-3 text complexity band independently and proficiently.

GRADE 4 MATH

CCSS.MATH.CONTENT.4.OA.A.2 Multiply or divide to solve word problems involving multiplicative comparison, e.g., by using drawings and equations with a symbol for the unknown number to represent the problem, distinguishing multiplicative comparison from additive comparison

CCSS.MATH.CONTENT.4.OA.A.3 Solve multistep word problems posed with whole numbers and having whole-number answers using the four operations, including problems in which remainders must be interpreted. Represent these problems using equations with a letter standing for the unknown quantity. Assess the reasonableness of answers using mental computation and estimation strategies including rounding.

CCSS.MATH.CONTENT.4.OA.B.4 Find all factor pairs for a whole number in the range 1-100. Recognize that a whole number is a multiple of each of its factors. Determine whether a given whole number in the range 1-100 is a multiple of a given one-digit number. Determine whether a given whole number in the range 1-100 is prime or composite.

CCSS.MATH.CONTENT.4.OA.C.5 Generate a number or shape pattern that follows a given rule. Identify apparent features of the pattern that were not explicit in the rule itself.

CCSS.MATH.CONTENT.4.NBT.B.4 Fluently add and subtract multi-digit whole numbers using the standard algorithm.

CCSS.MATH.CONTENT.4.NBT.B.5 Multiply a whole number of up to four digits by a one-digit whole number and multiply two two-digit numbers, using strategies based on place value and the properties of operations. Illustrate and explain the calculation by using equations, rectangular arrays, and/or area models.

CCSS.MATH.CONTENT.4.NBT.B.6 Find whole-number quotients and remainders with up to four-digit dividends and one-digit divisors, using strategies based on place value, the properties of operations, and/or the relationship between multiplication and division. Illustrate and explain the calculation by using equations, rectangular arrays, and/or area models.

CCSS.MATH.CONTENT.4.MD.A.2 Use the four operations to solve word problems involving distances, intervals of time, liquid volumes, masses of objects, and money, including problems involving simple fractions or decimals, and problems that require expressing measurements given in a larger unit in terms of a smaller unit. Represent measurement quantities using diagrams such as number line diagrams that feature a measurement scale.

GRADE 4 READING: LITERATURE

CCSS.ELA-LITERACY.RL.4.1 Refer to details and examples in a text when explaining what the text says explicitly and when drawing inferences from the text.

CCSS.ELA-LITERACY.RL.4.2 Determine a theme of a story, drama, or poem from details in the text; summarize the text.

CCSS.ELA-LITERACY.RL.4.3 Describe in depth a character, setting, or event in a story or drama, drawing on specific details in the text (e.g., a character's thoughts, words, or actions).